SIMPLE
MEDITERRANEAN
COOKING

SIMPLE MEDITERRANEAN COOKING

13-Digit ISBN: 978-1-64643-274-5
10-Digit ISBN: 1-64643-274-6

This book may be ordered by mail from the publisher. Please include $5.99 for postage and handling. Please support your local bookseller first!

Books published by Cider Mill Press Book Publishers are available at special discounts for bulk purchases in the United States by corporations, institutions, and other organizations. For more information, please contact the publisher.

Cider Mill Press Book Publishers
"Where good books are ready for press"
PO Box 454
12 Spring Street
Kennebunkport, Maine 04046

Visit us online!
cidermillpress.com

Typography: Filson Pro, Priori Sans OT

Image Credits: Pages 11, 14-15, 19, 20, 24-25, 31, 39, 42-43, 46-47, 51, 54-55, 57, 58, 65, 69, 70, 81, 86-87, 90-91, 94, 105, 107, 110-111, 113, 114, 117, 119, 128-129, 131, 134-135, 138-139, 140, 143, 144, 147, 149, 156, 159, 163, 167, and 182 courtesy of Cider Mill Press. All other images used under official license from Shutterstock.com.

Printed in China

Front cover image: Lamb Meatballs, see page 30; Tzatziki, see page 21

1 2 3 4 5 6 7 8 9 0
First Edition

SIMPLE
MEDITERRANEAN
COOKING

OVER 75 NOURISHING RECIPES CELEBRATING SOUTHERN EUROPEAN, NORTH AFRICAN, AND MIDDLE EASTERN FLAVORS

CIDER MILL PRESS

BOOK PUBLISHERS

KENNEBUNKPORT, MAINE

CONTENTS

INTRODUCTION

Spanning 21 countries, three continents, and regions as disparate as North Africa, the Levant, Catalonia, and Provence, the Mediterranean is a region unlike any other—particularly when it comes to cuisine.

This book is a vibrant conversation between the area's many cultures and perspectives. It celebrates what is unique to each, while also capturing the flair for using simple, straightforward methods to produce dynamic flavors that unites them. By leaning heavily upon the wonderful produce available in the region, this flair results in dishes that are as nutritious as they are delectable, a rare combination that has made *Mediterranean* a buzzword in wellness and weight-loss circles over the last decade.

Though this is not a dieting book, there is no avoiding the reality that emulating the Mediterranean approach to eating—a prevalence of vegetables, fruits, whole grains, seafood, and olive oil, only occasional encounters with poultry and beef, and a complete avoidance of seed oils and processed foods—will keep the pounds off, and help you feel better in general. At a time when a number of countries are having issues with obesity and chronic disease, Mediterranean cuisine's effortless ability to improve one's health has taken on an almost mystical air.

But the rush to brand the food of the Mediterranean as an antidote to modernity's ills paints an incomplete picture of the cuisine, excising the pasta and bread that make up a not-insignificant part of people's diets in the region. It is not that the people of the Mediterranean have unlocked the secrets of which foods to eat and which to ignore. Instead, the mystique is tied to the fact that they continue to follow the principles that carried humanity for so long—eat what is plentiful locally, and enjoy everything in moderation. Such an approach is not a cure-all, but it will supply your diet with far more balance, significantly broaden your palate, and connect you with a way of life that has enriched the people of the Mediterranean for millennia.

APPETIZERS & SNACKS

When the food of the Mediterranean is mentioned, many find their mind turning to preparations featured in this chapter—hummus, baba ghanoush, and, falafel, to name a few. As with so many of our immediate associations today, this one is due in part to the global marketplace making these dishes available throughout the world. But it is also because these small, delicious bites are perfect expressions of the region's culinary philosophy—amplifying the very best aspects of a single ingredient, and remaining straightforward while building dynamic flavors.

YIELD: **20 SERVINGS**

ACTIVE TIME: **1 HOUR**

TOTAL TIME: **24 HOURS**

Hummus

INGREDIENTS

2 lbs. dried chickpeas

1 tablespoon baking soda

12 cups room-temperature water

12 cups vegetable stock

1 cup tahini paste

2 tablespoons Za'atar (see page 92)

2 tablespoons sumac

2 tablespoons cumin

2 tablespoons kosher salt

2 tablespoons black pepper

2 garlic cloves, grated

½ bunch of fresh cilantro, roughly chopped

1 cup extra-virgin olive oil

1 cup sesame oil

1 cup ice water

½ cup fresh lemon juice

DIRECTIONS

1   Place the chickpeas, baking soda, and room-temperature water in a large saucepan, stir, and cover. Let the chickpeas soak overnight at room temperature.

2   Drain the chickpeas and rinse them. Place them in a large saucepan, add the stock, and bring to a steady simmer. Cook until the chickpeas are quite tender, about 1 hour.

3   In a blender or food processor, combine all of the remaining ingredients and puree until achieving a perfectly smooth, creamy sauce; the ice water is the key to getting the correct consistency.

4   Add the warm, drained chickpeas to the tahini mixture and blend until the hummus is perfectly smooth and not at all grainy, occasionally stopping to scrape down the sides of the bowl. This blending process may take 3 minutes; remain patient and keep going until the mixture is very creamy and fluffy, adding water as necessary to make the hummus move.

5   Taste, adjust the seasoning as necessary, and enjoy.

YIELD: **8 SERVINGS**

ACTIVE TIME: **30 MINUTES**

TOTAL TIME: **I HOUR**

Beet Chips

INGREDIENTS

4 cups canola oil

3 beets, rinsed well and dried

Salt and pepper, to taste

DIRECTIONS

1   Place the canola oil in a Dutch oven and warm it to 375°F. Line a baking sheet with paper towels and set a cooling rack in it.

2   Cut the root end from the beets and use a mandoline to cut the beets into ⅛-inch-thick slices.

3   Working in batches to avoid crowding the pot, gently slip the beets into the hot oil and fry until they are browned and stop bubbling and sizzling, 3 to 4 minutes. Remove the chips with a slotted spoon, season them with salt and pepper, and let them cool—they will crisp up as they do.

YIELD: **12 SERVINGS**

ACTIVE TIME: **15 MINUTES**

TOTAL TIME: **1 HOUR AND 15 MINUTES**

Baba Ghanoush

INGREDIENTS

2 large eggplants, halved

4 garlic cloves, smashed

4 teaspoons fresh lemon juice, plus more to taste

1½ teaspoons kosher salt, plus more to taste

½ cup tahini paste

¼ cup pomegranate seeds

2 teaspoons finely chopped fresh parsley

¼ cup extra-virgin olive oil

Pita Bread (see page 34), for serving

DIRECTIONS

1 Preheat the oven to 400°F. Place the eggplants on a baking sheet, cut side up, and roast until they have collapsed, about 50 minutes. Remove the eggplants from the oven and let them cool for 10 minutes.

2 Scoop the flesh of the eggplants into a food processor and discard the skins. Add the garlic, lemon juice, salt, and tahini and blitz until the mixture is smooth and creamy, about 1 minute. Taste and add more lemon juice and salt as necessary.

3 Transfer to a bowl, top with the pomegranate seeds, parsley, and olive oil, and serve with the Pita Bread.

Baba Ghanoush, see page 13

YIELD: **12 SERVINGS**
ACTIVE TIME: **15 MINUTES**
TOTAL TIME: **30 MINUTES**

Keftes de Espinaca

INGREDIENTS

½ cup plus 1 tablespoon avocado oil

1 onion, minced

½ teaspoon grated garlic

10 oz. fresh spinach

1 large egg

1 cup mashed potatoes

½ cup bread crumbs

1 teaspoon kosher salt

¼ teaspoon black pepper

Pinch of cayenne pepper

DIRECTIONS

1   Place the tablespoon of avocado oil in a large skillet and warm it over medium heat. Add the onion and cook, stirring frequently, until it starts to soften, about 5 minutes.

2   Add the garlic and cook until fragrant, about 1 minute. Add half of the spinach, cover the pan, and cook until the spinach has wilted. Add the remaining spinach, cover the pan again, and cook until all of the spinach has wilted.

3   Transfer the mixture to a fine-mesh strainer and gently press down on the mixture to remove excess moisture. Transfer the mixture to a cutting board and roughly chop it.

4   Place the mixture in a mixing bowl. Add the remaining ingredients and stir until thoroughly combined. Form ¼-cup portions of the mixture into patties and place them on a parchment-lined baking sheet.

5   Place the remaining avocado oil in the skillet and warm it to 365°F. Working in batches to avoid crowding the pan, slip the patties into the hot oil and fry until brown on both sides, about 8 minutes. Transfer the keftes to a paper towel-lined plate to drain before serving.

Tiropitakia

INGREDIENTS

½ lb. feta cheese

1 cup grated kefalotyri cheese

¼ cup finely chopped fresh parsley

2 eggs, beaten

Black pepper, to taste

1 (1 lb.) package of frozen phyllo dough, thawed

1 cup unsalted butter, melted

DIRECTIONS

1   Place the feta in a mixing bowl and break it up with a fork. Add the kefalotyri, parsley, eggs, and pepper and stir to combine. Set the mixture aside.

2   Place one sheet of the phyllo dough on a large sheet of parchment paper. Gently brush the sheet with some of the melted butter, place another sheet on top, and brush this with more of the butter. Cut the phyllo dough into 2-inch-wide strips, place 1 teaspoon of the filling at the end of the strip closest to you, and fold one corner over to make a triangle. Fold the strip up until the filling is completely covered. Repeat with the remaining sheets of phyllo dough and filling.

3   Preheat the oven to 350°F and coat a baking sheet with some of the melted butter. Place the pastries on the baking sheet and bake in the oven until golden brown, about 15 minutes. Remove the tiropitakia from the oven and let cool briefly before serving.

YIELD: **2 CUPS**

ACTIVE TIME: **5 MINUTES**

TOTAL TIME: **1 HOUR AND 5 MINUTES**

Tzatziki

INGREDIENTS

1 cup plain full-fat yogurt

¾ cup seeded and minced cucumber

1 garlic clove, minced

Juice from 1 lemon wedge

Salt and white pepper, to taste

Fresh dill, finely chopped, to taste

DIRECTIONS

1 Place the yogurt, cucumber, garlic, and lemon juice in a mixing bowl and stir to combine. Taste and season with salt and pepper. Stir in the dill.

2 Place in the refrigerator and chill for 1 hour before serving.

YIELD: **1 CUP**
ACTIVE TIME: **15 MINUTES**
TOTAL TIME: **1 HOUR**

Sweet Potato & Tahini Dip with Spiced Honey

INGREDIENTS

Extra-virgin olive oil, as needed

1 sweet potato, halved

1 yellow onion, quartered

2 large garlic cloves

¼ cup tahini paste

1 teaspoon fresh lemon juice

½ teaspoon kosher salt

2 tablespoons honey

½ teaspoon ancho chile powder

1 tablespoon chopped pistachios, for garnish

DIRECTIONS

1   Preheat the oven to 400°F and coat a baking sheet with olive oil. Place the sweet potato, cut side down, and the onion on the baking sheet. Place the garlic cloves in a small piece of aluminum foil, sprinkle a few drops of oil on them, wrap them up, and place on the baking sheet.

2   Place the baking sheet in the oven and roast for approximately 20 minutes, then remove the garlic. Roast the sweet potato and onion until the sweet potato is very tender, another 10 minutes or so. Remove from the oven and let cool.

3   Scoop the sweet potato's flesh into a food processor. Add the roasted onion, garlic, tahini, lemon juice, and salt. Pulse until the mixture is a smooth paste. Taste and adjust the seasoning as necessary.

4   Place the honey in a very small pot and warm it over low heat. Add the ancho chile powder, remove the pan from heat, and let it sit for a few minutes.

5   Place the puree in a shallow bowl and make a well in the center. Pour some of spiced honey in the well, garnish with the chopped pistachios, and enjoy.

YIELD: **4 SERVINGS**

ACTIVE TIME: **30 MINUTES**

TOTAL TIME: **2 HOURS**

Falafel

INGREDIENTS

1 (14 oz.) can of chickpeas, drained and rinsed

½ red onion, chopped

1 cup fresh parsley, chopped

1 cup fresh cilantro, chopped

3 bunches of scallions, trimmed and chopped

1 jalapeño chile pepper, stem and seeds removed, chopped

3 garlic cloves

1 teaspoon cumin

1 teaspoon kosher salt, plus more to taste

½ teaspoon cardamom

¼ teaspoon black pepper

2 tablespoons chickpea flour

½ teaspoon baking soda

Canola oil, as needed

Hummus (see page 10), for serving

Tahini Sauce (see page 95), for serving

DIRECTIONS

1 Line a baking sheet with parchment paper. Place all of the ingredients, except for the canola oil, in a food processor and blitz until pureed.

2 Scoop ¼-cup portions of the puree onto the baking sheet and place it in the refrigerator for 1 hour.

3 Add canola oil to a Dutch oven until it is 2 inches deep and warm it to 320°F over medium heat.

4 Working in batches, add the falafel to the oil and fry, turning occasionally, until they are golden brown, about 6 minutes. Transfer the cooked falafel to a paper towel–lined plate to drain.

5 When all of the falafel have been cooked, serve with the Hummus and Tahini Sauce.

Falafel, see page 23

Labneh

INGREDIENTS

4 cups full-fat Greek yogurt

½ teaspoon kosher salt

1 tablespoon extra-virgin olive oil

2 teaspoons Za'atar (see page 92)

DIRECTIONS

1 Place the yogurt in a large bowl and season it with the salt; the salt helps pull out excess whey, giving you a creamier, thicker labneh.

2 Place a fine-mesh strainer on top of a medium-sized bowl. Line the strainer with cheesecloth or a linen towel, letting a few inches hang over the side of the strainer. Spoon the seasoned yogurt into the cheesecloth and gently wrap the sides over the top of the yogurt, protecting it from being exposed to air in the refrigerator.

3 Store everything in the refrigerator for 24 to 48 hours, discarding the whey halfway through if the bowl beneath the strainer becomes too full.

4 Remove the labneh from the cheesecloth and store it in an airtight container.

5 To serve, drizzle the olive oil over the labneh and sprinkle the Za'atar on top.

YIELD: **2 SERVINGS**
ACTIVE TIME: **15 MINUTES**
TOTAL TIME: **30 MINUTES**

Scallop Ceviche

INGREDIENTS

1 teaspoon honey

½ teaspoon pomegranate molasses

Juice of 1 lime

Splash of white vinegar

Pinch of kosher salt

½ shallot, diced

1 tablespoon sliced scallions

2 fresh mint leaves, chopped

1 teaspoon chopped jalapeño chile pepper

6 large sea scallops, rinsed, feet removed

DIRECTIONS

1   In a mixing bowl, combine the honey, pomegranate molasses, lime juice, and white vinegar. Add the salt, shallot, scallions, mint, and jalapeño to the bowl, mix well, and let the mixture rest for 15 minutes.

2   Using a sharp knife, cut the scallops into ⅛-inch-thick slices. Add the scallops to the marinade and gently stir to coat. In a minute or two, the scallops will cure and turn fully white. Enjoy immediately.

YIELD: **2 SERVINGS**
ACTIVE TIME: **25 MINUTES**
TOTAL TIME: **25 MINUTES**

Fried Feta

INGREDIENTS

1 cup all-purpose flour

1 teaspoon kosher salt

1 teaspoon baking powder

1 cup water

Canola oil, as needed

1 block of feta cheese
(½-inch-thick)

1 teaspoon extra-virgin
olive oil

1 cup grape tomatoes

Leaves from ½ head of
romaine lettuce

1 tablespoon balsamic glaze

DIRECTIONS

1 Place the flour, salt, baking powder, and water in
a small bowl and whisk until the mixture is smooth.

2 Add canola oil to a small saucepan until it is about
1 inch deep and warm it over medium-high heat.

3 Carefully dip the block of feta in the batter until it
is completely coated.

4 Submerge half of the feta in the oil for 5 seconds,
then release it so that it floats. Fry for 1½ minutes
on each side, while keeping a close eye on the feta;
if the batter doesn't seal the feta will ooze out, and
this won't work. Once the feta has browned, remove
from the oil and set it on a cooling rack.

5 Place the olive oil in a medium skillet and warm it
over high heat. Add the tomatoes and cook until
they start to blister, 2 to 3 minutes. Add the lettuce
leaves and brown them for about 1 minute. Remove
the pan from heat.

6 To serve, place the lettuce in a shallow bowl, scatter
the tomatoes on top, and nestle the fried block
of feta on top. Drizzle the balsamic glaze over the
cheese and enjoy.

YIELD: **4 SERVINGS**
ACTIVE TIME: **20 MINUTES**
TOTAL TIME: **40 MINUTES**

Lamb Meatballs

INGREDIENTS

1 lb. ground lamb

1 white onion, grated

½ cup bread crumbs

1 egg

2 garlic cloves, minced

¼ cup fresh parsley, chopped

¼ cup fresh cilantro, chopped

¼ teaspoon cayenne pepper

¼ teaspoon red pepper flakes

Salt and pepper, to taste

2 tablespoons extra-virgin olive oil

DIRECTIONS

1 Place all of the ingredients, except for the olive oil, in a mixing bowl and work the mixture with your hands until combined. Form the mixture into 1-inch meatballs, place them on a plate, and chill them in the freezer for 15 minutes.

2 Place the olive oil in a large skillet and warm it over medium heat. Add the meatballs to the pan and cook, turning occasionally, until they are browned all over and cooked through, about 12 minutes. Let the meatballs cool slightly before serving.

Marinated Olives

INGREDIENTS

1½ lbs. assorted olives

2 teaspoons lightly cracked coriander seeds

1 teaspoon lightly cracked fennel seeds

¾ cup extra-virgin olive oil

2 tablespoons red wine vinegar

4 garlic cloves, sliced thin

1½ teaspoons chopped fresh rosemary

1½ teaspoons fresh thyme

4 bay leaves, torn

1 small dried red chile pepper, stem and seeds removed, chopped

2 strips of lemon zest

DIRECTIONS

1 Rinse any dark olives under cold water so their juices don't discolor the other olives. Place all of the olives in a colander and drain them. Transfer the olives to a wide-mouthed jar and set them aside.

2 Warm a dry skillet over medium-high heat. Add the coriander and fennel seeds and toast until very fragrant, about 2 minutes, stirring occasionally. Add the olive oil and vinegar and cook for 1 minute.

3 Remove the pan from heat and add all of the remaining ingredients. Stir to combine and let the mixture cool completely.

4 Pour the marinade over the olives, cover, and shake the jar so that the olives are evenly coated.

5 Chill the olives in the refrigerator for 2 hours before serving. If preparing the olives a few days ahead of time, shake the jar daily to redistribute the seasonings.

YIELD: **8 SERVINGS**

ACTIVE TIME: **1 HOUR**

TOTAL TIME: **3 HOURS**

Pita Bread

INGREDIENTS

1 cup lukewarm water (90°F)

1 tablespoon active dry yeast

1 tablespoon sugar

1¾ cups all-purpose flour, plus more as needed

1 cup whole wheat flour

1 tablespoon kosher salt

DIRECTIONS

1 In a large mixing bowl, combine the water, yeast, and sugar. Let the mixture sit until it starts to foam, about 10 minutes.

2 Add the flours and salt to the mixing bowl and work the mixture until it comes together as a smooth dough. Cover the bowl with a linen towel and let it rise for about 15 minutes.

3 Preheat the oven to 500°F and place a baking stone on the floor of the oven.

4 Divide the dough into eight pieces and form them into balls. Place the balls on a flour-dusted work surface, press them down, and roll them until they are about ¼ inch thick.

5 Working with one pita at a time, place the pita on the baking stone and bake until it is puffy and brown, about 8 minutes.

6 Remove the pita from the oven and serve warm or at room temperature.

SALADS & SIDES

While the inhabitants of Mediterranean are magnificent at using time, the region's surfeit of quality produce, and centuries of accrued knowledge to create dishes that are exceptionally wholesome and flavorful, this powerful alignment is not always available. At times, all you have time for is tossing a protein in a skillet, in the oven, or on the grill. You don't have to turn your back on the Mediterranean completely, though. While your piece of chicken or fish is cooking, simply whip up one of these vegetable-forward preparations to round out your table and remain in touch with the balanced approach to eating that has long been second nature in the region.

YIELD: **4 SERVINGS**

ACTIVE TIME: **30 MINUTES**

TOTAL TIME: **I HOUR**

Panzanella

INGREDIENTS

4 cups cubed crusty bread

6 tablespoons extra-virgin olive oil

Salt and pepper, to taste

2 tablespoons red wine vinegar

2 tablespoons chopped fresh basil

2 tablespoons chopped fresh oregano

1 lb. cherry tomatoes, halved

1 (14 oz.) can of cannellini beans, drained and rinsed

½ red onion, sliced thin

4 cups baby arugula

Parmesan cheese, shaved, for garnish

DIRECTIONS

1   Preheat the oven to 375°F. Place the bread and 2 tablespoons of the olive oil in a mixing bowl, season the mixture with salt and pepper, and toss to coat. Place the bread on a baking sheet, place it in the oven, and bake until it is golden brown, 8 to 10 minutes, stirring frequently. Remove the bread from the oven and let it cool.

2   Place the vinegar in a salad bowl. While whisking, slowly drizzle in the remaining olive oil. As this is a split vinaigrette, the oil will not emulsify. Add the herbs, tomatoes, beans, and onion to the vinaigrette and toss to coat.

3   Add the bread and baby arugula to the salt bowl, stir gently until combined, and season the salad with salt and pepper. Garnish with the Parmesan and enjoy.

YIELD: **4 SERVINGS**

ACTIVE TIME: **15 MINUTES**

TOTAL TIME: **40 MINUTES**

Bamies

INGREDIENTS

2 tablespoons extra-virgin olive oil

1 onion, chopped

1 lb. okra, rinsed well and chopped

1 potato, peeled and minced

1 garlic clove, minced

2 tomatoes, chopped

3 tablespoons white wine

½ cup vegetable stock

2 tablespoons chopped fresh parsley

2 teaspoons sugar

Salt, to taste

Feta cheese, crumbled, for garnish

DIRECTIONS

1 Place the olive oil in a medium skillet and warm it over medium heat. Add the onion and cook, stirring occasionally, until it starts to brown, about 8 minutes.

2 Add the okra and potato and cook, stirring frequently, until they start to brown, about 5 minutes.

3 Add the garlic and cook for 1 minute. Add the tomatoes, wine, stock, parsley, and sugar and stir to incorporate.

4 Cook until the tomatoes have collapsed and the okra and potato are tender, about 8 minutes.

5 Season with salt, garnish with feta, and enjoy.

YIELD: **4 SERVINGS**
ACTIVE TIME: **20 MINUTES**
TOTAL TIME: **20 MINUTES**

Grapefruit & Fennel Salad

INGREDIENTS

½ white onion

2 fennel stalks, fronds removed and reserved

1 apple

1 teaspoon chopped fresh dill

1 teaspoon chopped fresh mint

1 tablespoon chopped fresh parsley

1 tablespoon honey

3 tablespoons white vinegar

1 grapefruit

1 jalapeño chile pepper, stem and seeds removed, sliced thin

DIRECTIONS

1 Using a mandoline or a sharp knife, cut the onion, fennel stalks, and apple into very thin slices. Chop the fennel fronds. Place these items in a bowl.

2 Add the fresh herbs, honey, and white vinegar and toss to combine.

3 Trim the top and bottom from the grapefruit and then cut along the contour of the fruit to remove the pith and peel. Cut one segment, lengthwise, between the pulp and the membrane. Make a similar slice on the other side of the segment and then remove the pulp. Set aside and repeat with the remaining segments. This technique is known as "supreming," and can be used for all citrus fruits.

4 Add the segments to the salad bowl along with the jalapeño, toss to combine, and enjoy.

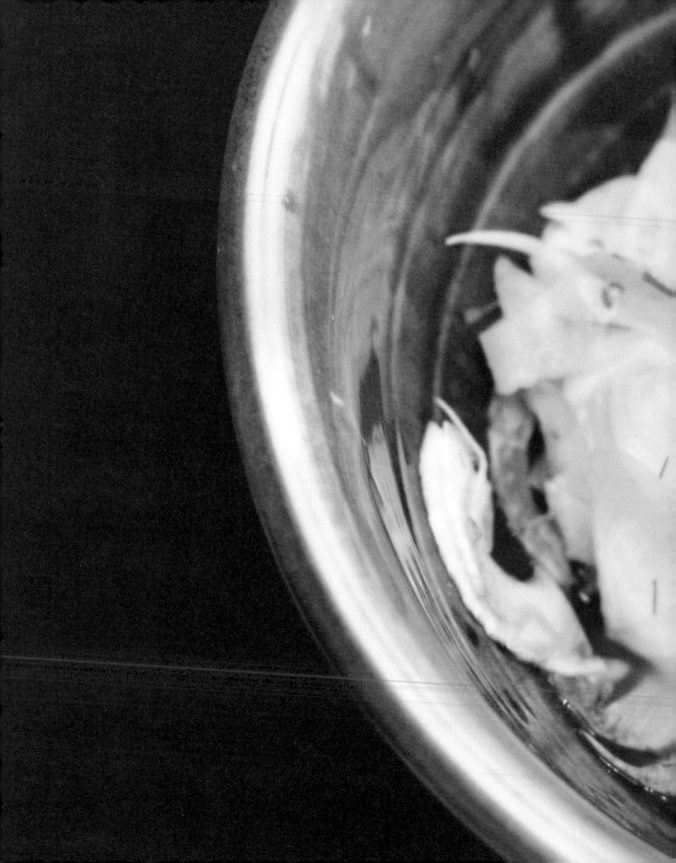

Grapefruit & Fennel Salad, see page 41

YIELD: **6 SERVINGS**

ACTIVE TIME: **15 MINUTES**

TOTAL TIME: **2 HOURS AND 30 MINUTES**

Lentil Salad

INGREDIENTS

1 cup lentils, picked over and rinsed

2½ tablespoons white wine vinegar

3 garlic cloves, minced

1 teaspoon herbes de Provence

1 bay leaf

Salt and pepper, to taste

1 (14 oz.) can of chickpeas, drained and rinsed

¾ lb. cherry tomatoes, halved

1 red onion, sliced

½ cup fresh parsley, chopped

¼ cup extra-virgin olive oil

2 cups baby spinach

½ cup crumbled feta cheese

DIRECTIONS

1   Place 4 cups water, lentils, 1 tablespoon of the vinegar, the garlic, herbes de Provence, and bay leaf in a slow cooker and season with salt. Cover and cook on high until the lentils are tender, about 2 hours.

2   Drain the lentils, discard the bay leaf, transfer to a large salad bowl, and let the lentils cool completely.

3   Stir in all of the remaining ingredients, except for the pepper and feta, and toss to combine. Season with salt and pepper, sprinkle the feta on top of the salad, and enjoy.

YIELD: **4 SERVINGS**

ACTIVE TIME: **30 MINUTES**

TOTAL TIME: **1 HOUR AND 30 MINUTES**

Turkish Eggplant Salad

INGREDIENTS

2 large eggplants

2 tablespoons extra-virgin olive oil

3 tomatoes, diced

1 white onion, julienned

4 garlic cloves, minced

1 tablespoon paprika

1 teaspoon kosher salt

1 teaspoon cumin

1 teaspoon cayenne pepper

½ cup chopped fresh parsley

DIRECTIONS

1   Preheat the oven to 450°F. Poke a few holes in the eggplants, place them on a baking sheet, and place them in the oven. Roast until completely tender and starting to collapse, 40 minutes to 1 hour. Remove the eggplants from the oven and let them cool completely.

2   Place the oil in a large skillet and warm it over high heat. Add the tomatoes and onion and cook until the onion is translucent, about 4 minutes. Add the remaining ingredients, except for the parsley, and cook for approximately 20 minutes, stirring occasionally. Transfer the mixture to a mixing bowl.

3   Halve the eggplants and scoop the flesh into the tomato mixture. Stir to combine, adding the parsley as you go. Let the mixture cool to room temperature before serving.

Turkish Eggplant Salad, see page 45

Minty Pickled Cucumbers

INGREDIENTS

½ cup sugar

½ cup water

½ cup rice wine vinegar

2 tablespoons dried mint

1 tablespoon coriander seeds

1 tablespoon mustard seeds

2 cucumbers, sliced

DIRECTIONS

1 Place all of the ingredients, except for the cucumbers, in a small saucepan and bring to a boil, stirring to dissolve the sugar.

2 Place the cucumbers in a large mason jar. Remove the pan from heat and pour the brine over the cucumbers.

3 Let cool completely before using or storing in the refrigerator, where the pickles will keep for 1 week.

YIELD: **4 SERVINGS**

ACTIVE TIME: **45 MINUTES**

TOTAL TIME: **2 DAYS**

Pickled Green Beans

INGREDIENTS

1 lb. green beans, trimmed

2 tablespoons chopped fresh dill

2 garlic cloves, minced

1 tablespoon kosher salt

1 tablespoon sugar

2 cups white vinegar

1 tablespoon extra-virgin olive oil

1 tablespoon honey

DIRECTIONS

1   Place the green beans, dill, garlic, salt, and sugar in a large mason jar. Pour the vinegar over the mixture, cover the jar, and shake to combine. Chill the green beans in the refrigerator for 48 hours.

2   Preheat the oven to 450°F. Remove the green beans from the liquid and place them on a baking sheet. Drizzle the olive oil over them and toss to coat.

3   Place the green beans in the oven and roast until browned, about 20 minutes.

4   Remove the green beans from the oven, drizzle the honey over them, and enjoy.

YIELD: **16 SERVINGS**
ACTIVE TIME: **30 MINUTES**
TOTAL TIME: **30 MINUTES**

Crunchy Pomegranate Salad

INGREDIENTS

2 cups heavy cream

¼ cup sugar

2 teaspoons pure vanilla extract

2½ cups pomegranate seeds

2 apples, peeled, cored, and cubed

1 cup chopped pecans, toasted

DIRECTIONS

1   Place the cream in the work bowl of a stand mixer fitted with the whisk attachment and beat it until it starts to thicken.

2   Add the sugar and vanilla and beat until the mixture holds stiff peaks.

3   Fold in the pomegranate seeds and apples, sprinkle the pecans over the top, and serve immediately.

YIELD: **2 SERVINGS**
ACTIVE TIME: **15 MINUTES**
TOTAL TIME: **30 MINUTES**

Glazed Okra

INGREDIENTS

2 tablespoons extra-virgin olive oil

12 okra pods

1 teaspoon kosher salt

1 teaspoon black pepper

1 teaspoon brown sugar

1 teaspoon white vinegar

¼ cup crumbled goat cheese

DIRECTIONS

1 Place the olive oil in a large cast-iron pan and warm it over high heat. Add the okra, season it with salt and pepper, and cook until the okra is browned all over, turning it as necessary.

2 Remove the okra from the pan and set it aside. Turn off the heat but leave the pan on the stove.

3 Place the brown sugar and vinegar in the pan and stir until the mixture is syrupy.

4 Spread the goat cheese on a serving plate, arrange the okra in a line on top of it, drizzle the glaze over the top, and enjoy.

Glazed Okra, see page 53

YIELD: **2 SERVINGS**
ACTIVE TIME: **15 MINUTES**
TOTAL TIME: **15 MINUTES**

Moroccan Carrots

INGREDIENTS

2 large carrots, peeled

1 tablespoon avocado oil

1 tablespoon ras el hanout

2 teaspoons honey

2 teaspoons tahini paste

2 pinches of white sesame seeds, for garnish

DIRECTIONS

1   Cut the carrots into matchsticks that are approximately ½ inch wide and 3 inches long.

2   Place the avocado oil in a large skillet and warm it over high heat. Add the carrots to the pan, making sure to leave as much space between them as possible. Sprinkle the ras el hanout over the carrots and sear them until lightly charred all over, about 6 minutes, turning them as necessary.

3   Transfer the carrots to a paper towel-lined plate to drain.

4   Divide the carrots between the serving plates and drizzle the honey and tahini over each portion. Garnish with the sesame seeds and enjoy.

YIELD: **2 SERVINGS**

ACTIVE TIME: **30 MINUTES**

TOTAL TIME: **1 HOUR AND 30 MINUTES**

Beets with Walnut Dukkah

INGREDIENTS

1 large beet, unpeeled

Pinch of kosher salt

1 tablespoon chopped walnuts

1 tablespoon chopped hazelnuts

1 teaspoon black pepper

1 teaspoon poppy seeds

1 teaspoon black sesame seeds

1 tablespoon avocado oil

¼ cup Labneh (see page 26)

1 cinnamon stick

DIRECTIONS

1   Place the beet and salt in a saucepan with at least 5 cups of water and bring to a boil. Cook the beet until a knife can easily pass through it, 30 to 40 minutes.

2   Drain the beet, run it under cold water, and peel off the skin and stem; it is easiest to do this while the beet is still hot.

3   Cut the peeled beet into ¾-inch cubes and set them aside.

4   Place the nuts in a resealable bag and use a rolling pin to crush them. Transfer to a small bowl, add the black pepper and seeds, and stir to combine. Set the mixture aside.

5   Place the avocado oil in a large skillet and warm it over high heat. Place the beet in the pan and sear until well browned all over, about 5 minutes, turning the beet as necessary. Transfer the beet to a paper towel–lined plate to drain.

6   To serve, spread the Labneh across a shallow bowl, pile the beet on top, and sprinkle the dukkah over the dish. Grate the cinnamon stick over the dish and enjoy.

YIELD: **4 SERVINGS**
ACTIVE TIME: **10 MINUTES**
TOTAL TIME: **10 MINUTES**

Horiatiki Salad

INGREDIENTS

1 cucumber, peeled, seeds removed, sliced into half-moons

1 cup cherry tomatoes, halved

1 cup crumbled feta cheese

1 onion, chopped

½ cup Kalamata olives, pits removed, sliced

1 teaspoon dried oregano

½ cup extra-virgin olive oil

Salt and pepper, to taste

DIRECTIONS

1 Place the cucumber, cherry tomatoes, feta, onion, olives, and oregano in a mixing bowl and stir gently until combined.

2 Drizzle the olive oil over the salad, season with salt and pepper, gently toss to combine, and enjoy.

YIELD: **4 CUPS**
ACTIVE TIME: **15 MINUTES**
TOTAL TIME: **30 MINUTES**

Tabbouleh

INGREDIENTS

½ cup bulgur wheat

1½ cups boiling water

½ teaspoon kosher salt,
plus more to taste

½ cup fresh lemon juice

2 cups fresh parsley, chopped

1 cup peeled, deseeded,
and diced cucumber

2 tomatoes, diced

6 scallions, trimmed

1 cup fresh mint leaves,
chopped

2 tablespoons extra-virgin
olive oil

Black pepper, to taste

½ cup crumbled feta cheese

DIRECTIONS

1   Place the bulgur in a bowl and add the boiling water,
salt, and half of the lemon juice. Cover and let sit for
about 20 minutes, until the bulgur has absorbed all
of the liquid and is tender. Drain any excess liquid if
necessary. Let the bulgur cool completely.

2   When the bulgur has cooled, add the parsley,
cucumber, tomatoes, scallions, mint, olive oil, black
pepper, and remaining lemon juice and stir until
well combined.

3   Top with the feta and enjoy.

YIELD: **4 SERVINGS**
ACTIVE TIME: **20 MINUTES**
TOTAL TIME: **30 MINUTES**

Fava Beans with Pomegranates

DIRECTIONS

1 Place the onion, sumac, and red wine vinegar in a bowl, season with salt, and let the mixture sit until the onion turns bright red and becomes slightly pickled.

2 Place the avocado oil in a large saucepan and warm it over medium-low heat. Add the garlic and fava beans and cook, stirring occasionally, until the fava beans are bright green in color. Season with the sea salt, pepper, Za'atar, and lemon juice and stir to combine.

3 Remove the pan from heat and stir in the fresh herbs and pomegranate seeds.

4 Transfer to a serving bowl, garnish with the onions, pomegranate molasses, olive oil, and Labneh, and enjoy.

INGREDIENTS

½ red onion, sliced thin

1 teaspoon sumac

1 teaspoon red wine vinegar

½ teaspoon kosher salt, plus more to taste

2 tablespoons avocado oil

2 garlic cloves, chopped

1½ lbs. fresh young fava beans, pods and inner shells removed

¼ teaspoon black pepper

1 teaspoon Za'atar (see page 92)

Juice of ½ lemon

½ cup chopped fresh parsley

¼ cup chopped fresh dill

¼ cup fresh mint leaves

¼ cup pomegranate seeds

1 teaspoon pomegranate molasses, for garnish

2 tablespoons extra-virgin olive oil, for garnish

2 tablespoons Labneh (see page 26), for garnish

YIELD: **4 SERVINGS**

ACTIVE TIME: **30 MINUTES**

TOTAL TIME: **I HOUR**

Roasted Brussels Sprouts with Warm Honey Glaze

DIRECTIONS

1   Position a rack in the bottom third of the oven and set a rimmed baking sheet on it. Preheat the oven to 450°F.

2   In a large bowl, combine the Brussels sprouts and oil, toss to coat, and season with salt and pepper.

3   Carefully remove the baking sheet from the oven. Using tongs, arrange the Brussels sprouts, cut side down, on the hot baking sheet. Place the pan back on the low rack and roast the Brussels sprouts until they are tender and deeply browned, 20 to 25 minutes.

4   While the Brussels sprouts are roasting, place the honey in a small saucepan and bring it to a simmer over medium-high heat. Reduce the heat to medium-low and cook, stirring frequently, until the honey is a deep amber color but not burnt (it will be foamy), about 3 minutes. Remove from heat, carefully add the vinegar and red pepper flakes, and stir until incorporated.

5   Place the saucepan back over medium heat, stir in the butter and ½ teaspoon salt, and cook, whisking constantly, until the glaze is glossy, bubbling, and has thickened, about 4 minutes.

6   Remove the Brussels sprouts from the oven, transfer them to a large bowl, and add the glaze. Toss to coat, top with the scallions and lemon zest, and enjoy.

INGREDIENTS

1½ lbs. Brussels sprouts, trimmed and halved

¼ cup avocado oil

½ teaspoon kosher salt, plus more to taste

Black pepper, to taste

¼ cup honey

⅓ cup sherry vinegar or red wine vinegar

¾ teaspoon crushed red pepper flakes

3 tablespoons unsalted butter

3 scallions, trimmed and sliced thin on a bias

1 teaspoon lemon zest

Romano Beans with Mustard Vinaigrette & Walnuts

INGREDIENTS

1 cup walnuts

Salt and pepper, to taste

3 lbs. Romano beans, trimmed

3 tablespoons red wine vinegar

2 tablespoons Dijon mustard

1 garlic clove, finely grated

2 tablespoons extra-virgin olive oil, plus more to taste

Zest of ½ lemon

¾ cup chopped fresh parsley

DIRECTIONS

1   Preheat the oven to 350°F. Place the walnuts on a rimmed baking sheet, place them in the oven, and toast until browned and fragrant, about 8 to 10 minutes, tossing halfway through.

2   Remove the walnuts from the oven and let them cool. When the walnuts have cooled slightly, chop them and set aside.

3   Bring salted water to a boil in a large saucepan and prepare an ice bath. Place the beans in the boiling water and cook until bright green and tender, 8 to 10 minutes. Using a slotted spoon, transfer them to the ice bath and let them cool. Drain, pat the beans dry, and set them aside.

4   Place the vinegar, mustard, garlic, and olive oil in a large mixing bowl and whisk until thoroughly combined. Let the dressing rest for 10 minutes.

5   Add the walnuts and beans to the dressing. Sprinkle the lemon zest and parsley over the beans, season with salt and pepper, and toss to coat. Transfer to a platter, drizzle more olive oil over the top, and enjoy.

Braised Leeks

INGREDIENTS

½ cup extra-virgin olive oil

6 large leeks, trimmed, rinsed well, and halved lengthwise

Salt and pepper, to taste

2 tablespoons avocado oil

4 shallots, chopped

2 garlic cloves, minced

1 teaspoon dried thyme

1 teaspoon lemon zest

½ cup white wine

2 cups vegetable stock

DIRECTIONS

1 Preheat the oven to 400°F. Place the olive oil in a large skillet and warm it over medium-high heat. Season the leeks with salt and pepper, place them in the pan, cut side down, and sear until golden brown, about 5 minutes.

2 Season the leeks with salt and pepper, turn them over, and cook until browned on that side, about 2 minutes. Transfer the leeks to a baking dish.

3 Place the avocado oil in the skillet and warm it over medium-high heat. Add the shallots and cook until they start to brown, about 5 minutes.

4 Add the garlic, thyme, lemon zest, salt, and pepper to the pan and cook until just fragrant, about 1 minute.

5 Add the wine and cook until it has reduced by half, about 10 minutes.

6 Add the stock and bring the mixture to a boil. Remove the pan from heat and pour the mixture over the leeks until they are almost, but not quite, submerged.

7 Place the dish in the oven and braise the leeks until tender, about 30 minutes.

8 Remove from the oven, transfer to a serving dish, and enjoy.

YIELD: **6 SERVINGS**
ACTIVE TIME: **20 MINUTES**
TOTAL TIME: **50 MINUTES**

Couscous with Seven Vegetables

INGREDIENTS

3 tablespoons avocado oil

1 large yellow onion, diced

Salt and pepper, to taste

2 garlic cloves, minced

2 tomatoes, seeds removed, diced

1 tablespoon tomato paste

2 teaspoons cumin

1 teaspoon paprika

1 teaspoon ground ginger

1 teaspoon cinnamon

¼ teaspoon cayenne pepper

2 red bell peppers, stems and seeds removed, chopped

2 zucchini, halved and chopped

Continued...

DIRECTIONS

1 Place the avocado oil in a Dutch oven and warm it over medium heat. Add the onion and cook, stirring occasionally, until it has softened, about 5 minutes.

2 Season the onion with salt and pepper, add the garlic and tomatoes, and cook, stirring frequently, until the tomatoes start to collapse, about 5 minutes. Stir in the tomato paste, cumin, paprika, ginger, cinnamon, and cayenne and cook, stirring frequently, until the mixture is fragrant, 2 to 3 minutes.

3 Add the peppers, zucchini, turnips, carrots, squash, and stock and bring to a boil. Reduce the heat, cover the pan, and simmer until the vegetables are tender, 10 to 15 minutes.

4 Remove the cover and add the chickpeas. Simmer until chickpeas are warmed through and the stew has thickened, 5 to 10 minutes.

5 Meanwhile, make the couscous according to the directions on the package.

6 Stir the ras el hanout into the stew, taste, and adjust the seasoning as necessary.

7 To serve, spread the couscous on a platter. Spoon the vegetable stew over the couscous, garnish with the parsley and slivered almonds, and enjoy.

2 to 3 small turnips, peeled
and chopped

1 bunch of carrots, trimmed,
peeled, and chopped

1 butternut squash, peeled
and cubed

4 cups vegetable stock

1 (14 oz.) can of chickpeas,
drained and rinsed

1 box of couscous

2 teaspoons ras el hanout

2 tablespoons chopped fresh
parsley, for garnish

Slivered almonds, for garnish

YIELD: **8 SERVINGS**

ACTIVE TIME: **15 MINUTES**

TOTAL TIME: **30 MINUTES**

Green Beans with Za'atar & Lemon

INGREDIENTS

¼ cup chicken stock

2 lbs. green beans, trimmed

2 tablespoons unsalted butter

1 tablespoon Za'atar (see page 92)

Zest of 1 lemon

Salt and pepper, to taste

DIRECTIONS

1 Place the stock in a large skillet and bring it to a simmer over medium-high heat. Add the green beans, cover the pan, and cook, tossing occasionally, until the green beans are just tender, 5 to 7 minutes.

2 Uncover the pan, add the butter, and toss to coat the green beans.

3 Remove the pan from heat and stir in the Za'atar and lemon zest. Season with salt and pepper and enjoy.

YIELD: **6 SERVINGS**
ACTIVE TIME: **10 MINUTES**
TOTAL TIME: **30 MINUTES**

Roasted Pepper Salad

INGREDIENTS

3 red bell peppers

2 yellow bell peppers

1 green bell pepper

½ cup plus 1 tablespoon avocado oil

½ onion, sliced thin

1 teaspoon white vinegar

¼ teaspoon kosher salt

⅛ teaspoon black pepper

½ teaspoon cumin

¼ bunch of fresh cilantro, chopped

DIRECTIONS

1 Roast the peppers on a grill or over the flame of a gas burner until they are charred all over and tender. Place the peppers in a baking dish, cover it with plastic wrap, and let them steam for 10 minutes.

2 Remove the charred skins and the seed pods from the peppers and discard them. Slice the roasted peppers into strips and set them aside.

3 Place 1 tablespoon of the avocado oil in a saucepan and warm it over medium heat. Add the onion and cook, stirring occasionally, until it has softened, about 5 minutes. Remove the pan from heat and let the onion cool.

4 Place the peppers, onion, remaining avocado oil, vinegar, salt, pepper, cumin, and cilantro in a bowl, stir until combined, and enjoy.

SAUCES, DRESSINGS & SEASONINGS

The bright and dynamic flavors offered by these simple pantry staples can lift a large percentage of one's work in the kitchen. Be generous about incorporating them into your other preparations—they are a worthy foundation to build a creative, varied, and unique approach upon.

YIELD: 1½ **CUPS**

ACTIVE TIME: **1 HOUR**

TOTAL TIME: **1 HOUR**

Dukkah

INGREDIENTS

1 head of garlic

1 large shallot

¾ cup extra-virgin olive oil

1 cup shelled raw pistachios

2 tablespoons coriander seeds

2 tablespoons black sesame seeds

2 tablespoons white sesame seeds

1½ tablespoons pink peppercorns

1 tablespoon Maldon sea salt

2 teaspoons sumac

2 teaspoons Aleppo pepper

1½ tablespoons dried mint

1½ tablespoons dried thyme

DIRECTIONS

1 Preheat the oven to 325°F.

2 Peel the garlic cloves, trim the ends of each clove, and slice them as thinly and evenly as you can. Trim the ends of the shallot, halve it lengthwise, and slice it as thin as possible.

3 Place the garlic and shallot in a cold skillet, add the olive oil, and cook over low heat until they are a deep, even golden brown, 30 to 40 minutes, stirring occasionally to make sure the heat circulates evenly. This long cook time allows them to build flavor without also becoming bitter, so don't try to speed it up with a higher flame.

4 While the garlic and shallot are cooking, place the pistachios on a baking sheet, place them in the oven, and roast until fragrant, 6 to 7 minutes. Remove the pistachios from the oven and let them cool.

5 Line a plate with paper towels. Strain the garlic and shallot over a clean bowl and spread them on the plate in an even layer. Wipe out the skillet and fill it with the reserved oil. Add the coriander seeds, black sesame seeds, and white sesame seeds. Toast, over low heat, until the seeds are crunchy and aromatic, about 8 minutes. Drain and place the seeds on the same plate as the shallot and garlic.

6 Place the shallot, garlic, and seeds in a large resealable plastic bag with the pistachios and the remaining ingredients. Pound the mixture with a rolling pin or mallet until everything is roughly crushed. Use immediately or store in an airtight container in the refrigerator.

Champagne Vinaigrette

INGREDIENTS

⅔ cup Champagne vinegar

¼ cup water

2 tablespoons Dijon mustard

½ teaspoon kosher salt

½ teaspoon black pepper

2 tablespoons honey

1½ cups extra-virgin olive oil

DIRECTIONS

1 Place all of the ingredients, except for the olive oil, in a bowl and whisk until well combined.

2 While whisking, add the oil in a slow stream until it has emulsified. Use immediately or store in the refrigerator.

YIELD: **2½ CUPS**

ACTIVE TIME: **5 MINUTES**

TOTAL TIME: **5 MINUTES**

Lemony Yogurt Sauce

INGREDIENTS

6 tablespoons fresh
lemon juice

1 garlic clove, grated

1 teaspoon kosher salt

1 teaspoon black pepper

2 cups full-fat Greek yogurt

DIRECTIONS

1 Place all of the ingredients in a mixing bowl and stir
until thoroughly combined. Use immediately or store
in the refrigerator.

YIELD: **2½ CUPS**
ACTIVE TIME: **10 MINUTES**
TOTAL TIME: **10 MINUTES**

Red Zhug

INGREDIENTS

4 Fresno chile peppers,
stems and seeds removed,
roughly chopped

2 cups fresh parsley

1 onion, quartered

5 garlic cloves

Juice of 1 lemon

1 tablespoon kosher salt

1 teaspoon cayenne pepper

1 tablespoon cumin

2 tablespoons paprika

¾ cup extra-virgin olive oil

DIRECTIONS

1   Place the chiles, parsley, onion, garlic, and lemon juice in a food processor and pulse until combined.

2   Add the salt, cayenne, cumin, and paprika, and, with the food processor on high, slowly pour in the olive oil. Blitz until the mixture is emulsified, adding water as needed to get the desired texture. Use immediately or store in the refrigerator.

Green Zhug

INGREDIENTS

4 jalapeño chile peppers, stems and seeds removed, roughly chopped

2 cups fresh parsley

¼ cup fresh cilantro

6 fresh mint leaves

1 onion, quartered

5 garlic cloves

Juice of 1 lemon

1 tablespoon kosher salt

½ cup extra-virgin olive oil

DIRECTIONS

1 Place the jalapeños, parsley, cilantro, mint, onion, garlic, and lemon juice in a food processor and pulse until combined.

2 Add the salt, and, with the food processor on high, slowly pour in the olive oil. Blitz until the mixture is emulsified, adding water as needed to get the desired texture. Use immediately or store in the refrigerator.

Green Zhug, see page 85

YIELD: **4 CUPS**

ACTIVE TIME: **30 MINUTES**

TOTAL TIME: **30 MINUTES**

Pomegranate Vinaigrette

INGREDIENTS

2 cups pomegranate juice

½ cup red wine vinegar

2 tablespoons Dijon mustard

2 tablespoons honey

1 tablespoon Za'atar
(see page 92)

2 teaspoons sumac

2 tablespoons kosher salt

1 tablespoon black pepper

1 tablespoon chopped
fresh oregano

1 tablespoon chopped
fresh basil

1 tablespoon chopped
fresh parsley

1 tablespoon chopped
fresh mint

3 cups extra-virgin olive oil

DIRECTIONS

1 Place the pomegranate juice in a small saucepan and bring it to a boil over medium-high heat. Boil until it has reduced to ¼ cup. Remove the pan from heat and let it cool.

2 Place the pomegranate reduction and the remaining ingredients, except for the olive oil, in a blender and puree until smooth.

3 With the blender on, drizzle in the oil. Puree until it has emulsified. Use immediately or store in the refrigerator.

YIELD: **5 CUPS**

ACTIVE TIME: **5 MINUTES**

TOTAL TIME: **10 MINUTES**

Chermoula Sauce

INGREDIENTS

1 tablespoon saffron threads

4 cups mayonnaise

1 tablespoon ras el hanout

1 tablespoon berbere seasoning

2 tablespoons Za'atar (see page 92)

1 tablespoon sumac

2 cups chopped fresh herbs (tarragon, parsley, chives, and cilantro recommended)

1 tablespoon dried oregano

1 tablespoon kosher salt

1 tablespoon black pepper

DIRECTIONS

1   Place the saffron in ¼ cup water and let it bloom. Remove the saffron from the water and reserve the liquid for another preparation (it's really good in a tomato sauce, for example)—using it in this sauce will make it too loose.

2   Place the saffron and the remaining ingredients in a large bowl and stir until thoroughly combined. Use immediately or transfer to an airtight container and store in the refrigerator.

Chermoula Sauce, see page 89

YIELD: 1½ **CUPS**
ACTIVE TIME: **5 MINUTES**
TOTAL TIME: **5 MINUTES**

Za'atar

INGREDIENTS

1 tablespoon cumin

1 tablespoon sumac

1 tablespoon thyme

2 teaspoons hemp seeds

2 teaspoons crushed toasted
sunflower seeds

2 tablespoons sesame seeds

2 tablespoons kosher salt

1 tablespoon black pepper

2 tablespoons chopped
fresh oregano

2 tablespoons chopped
fresh basil

2 tablespoons chopped
fresh parsley

1 tablespoon garlic powder

1 tablespoon onion powder

DIRECTIONS

1   Place all of the ingredients in a large bowl and stir
until thoroughly combined. Use immediately or store
in an airtight container.

Tahini Sauce

INGREDIENTS

5 oz. tahini paste

½ cup water

3 garlic cloves

1 teaspoon kosher salt

Juice of 1 lemon

Pinch of cumin

DIRECTIONS

1   Place the tahini and water in a food processor and pulse to combine. Let the mixture sit for 30 seconds.

2   Add the garlic, salt, lemon juice, and cumin. Puree on high for 2 to 3 minutes, until the sauce is creamy and smooth. Use immediately or store in the refrigerator.

YIELD: **4 CUPS**
ACTIVE TIME: **15 MINUTES**
TOTAL TIME: **45 MINUTES**

Tomato Sauce

INGREDIENTS

2 tablespoons avocado oil

1 large garlic clove, chopped

1 teaspoon grated
fresh ginger

1 cinnamon stick

1 (28 oz.) can of chopped
San Marzano tomatoes,
with their liquid

½ teaspoon cumin

¼ teaspoon coriander

⅛ teaspoon cayenne pepper

DIRECTIONS

1   Place the oil in a large saucepan and warm it over
medium heat. Add the garlic and ginger and cook,
stirring frequently, until fragrant, about 1 minute.

2   Add the cinnamon stick and cook for 30 seconds.
Add the remaining ingredients and bring the sauce
to a boil.

3   Reduce the heat and simmer the sauce until the flavor
has developed to your liking, about 30 minutes.

4   Remove the cinnamon stick from the sauce and use
as desired.

YIELD: **1 CUP**

ACTIVE TIME: **10 MINUTES**

TOTAL TIME: **1 HOUR**

Three-Pepper Harissa Sauce

INGREDIENTS

3 oz. guajillo chile peppers, stems and seeds removed, torn

1 oz. dried chipotle chile peppers, stems and seeds removed, torn

1 tablespoon nigella seeds

1 teaspoon coriander seeds

2 garlic cloves

1 tablespoon cumin

1 teaspoon kosher salt

½ teaspoon Aleppo pepper

½ cup extra-virgin olive oil

2 tablespoons white wine vinegar

DIRECTIONS

1 Place the guajillo and chipotle chiles in a large heatproof bowl and cover them with boiling water. Let the chiles soak until they have softened, 40 to 45 minutes.

2 Drain the chiles and set them aside.

3 Grind the nigella seeds and coriander seeds into a powder using a spice mill or a mortar and pestle. Transfer the powder to a food processor and add the garlic, cumin, salt, and Aleppo pepper. Pulse until the garlic is very finely chopped.

4 Add the chiles and pulse until they are chopped.

5 Add the oil and vinegar and pulse until the sauce is a chunky paste.

YIELD: **1 CUP**

ACTIVE TIME: **5 MINUTES**

TOTAL TIME: **5 MINUTES**

Salsa Verde

INGREDIENTS

1 cup fresh parsley

1 garlic clove

1 tablespoon fresh
lemon juice

1 tablespoon chopped fresh
rosemary

1 teaspoon kosher salt

1 strip of lemon zest

1 tablespoon capers, drained

½ teaspoon red pepper flakes

Black pepper, to taste

¼ cup extra-virgin olive oil

DIRECTIONS

1   Place all of the ingredients, except for the olive oil, in a food processor and puree until it is nearly smooth, scraping down the work bowl as needed.

2   With the food processor running, slowly drizzle in the olive oil and blitz until it has emulsified.

3   If not using immediately, refrigerate and let the sauce come to room temperature before serving.

SOUPS & STEWS

Outsiders tend to picture the Mediterranean as a temperate, sun-soaked region, a gloss that—between the French Riviera, Sicily, sunny old Athens, North Africa, and the Levant—is not far off the mark. As such, soup is not the dish that leaps to mind when one thinks of the food. But, remember—no cuisine is as focused on simplicity and comfort quite like the countries in this area. Considering this, it is only natural that these wonderful soups and stews number among the Mediterranean's many culinary treasures.

YIELD: **4 SERVINGS**

ACTIVE TIME: **30 MINUTES**

TOTAL TIME: **24 HOURS**

Dried Fava Bean Soup with Grilled Halloumi Cheese

INGREDIENTS

1½ cups dried fava beans, soaked overnight

6 cups vegetable or chicken stock

4 garlic cloves, minced

5 tablespoons extra-virgin olive oil

1 shallot, minced

Zest and juice of 1 lemon

Salt and pepper, to taste

2 tablespoons finely chopped fresh parsley

½ lb. Halloumi cheese, cut into 4 pieces

Lemon wedges, for serving

DIRECTIONS

1   Drain the fava beans and place them in a large saucepan with the stock and garlic. Bring to a boil, reduce the heat so that the soup simmers, cover, and cook until the beans are so tender that they are starting to fall apart, about 1 hour.

2   While the soup is simmering, place ¼ cup of the olive oil in a skillet and warm over medium heat. When the oil starts to shimmer, add the shallot and sauté until it starts to soften, about 5 minutes. Remove the pan from heat, stir in the lemon zest, and let the mixture sit for 1 hour.

3   Transfer the soup to a food processor and puree until smooth. Return the soup to a clean saucepan, season with salt and pepper, and bring it to a gentle simmer. Stir in the mixture in the skillet, the lemon juice, and the parsley, cook until heated through, and remove the soup from heat.

4   Warm a skillet over medium heat. Place the remaining olive oil in a small bowl, add the cheese, and toss to coat. Place the cheese in the pan and cook until browned on both sides, about 2 minutes per side. Serve the cheese and lemon wedges alongside the soup.

YIELD: **4 SERVINGS**

ACTIVE TIME: **30 MINUTES**

TOTAL TIME: **24 HOURS**

Chamin

INGREDIENTS

1½ tablespoons extra-virgin olive oil

1 small onion, chopped

5 garlic cloves, minced

¾ cup chopped parsnip

2 carrots, peeled and sliced

1 teaspoon cumin

¼ teaspoon turmeric

1½-inch piece of fresh ginger, peeled and minced

½ lb. beef brisket, trimmed and chopped

4 oz. lamb shoulder, trimmed and chopped

4 cups beef stock

½ cup chickpeas, soaked overnight and drained

1 small potato, peeled and chopped

1 small zucchini, sliced

Continued...

DIRECTIONS

1 Preheat the oven to 250°F. Place the olive oil in a Dutch oven and warm over medium heat. Add the onion, garlic, parsnip, carrots, cumin, turmeric, and ginger and cook, stirring continually, for 2 minutes.

2 Add the brisket and lamb and cook, stirring occasionally, until both are browned all over, about 8 minutes.

3 Add the stock and bring the soup to a simmer. Stir in the chickpeas, potato, zucchini, tomatoes, lentils, bay leaf, and cilantro. Cover the pot, place it in the oven, and cook until the meat is tender, about 1 hour.

4 Remove the stew from the oven and skim the fat from the top. Season with salt and pepper and ladle into warmed bowls. Garnish with the chiles and serve with the lemon wedges and rice.

½ lb. tomatoes, chopped

2 tablespoons brown lentils

1 bay leaf

½ bunch of fresh cilantro, chopped

Salt and pepper, to taste

Fresh chile peppers, stems and seeds removed, chopped, for garnish

Lemon wedges, for serving

Long-grain rice, cooked, for serving

YIELD: **4 SERVINGS**

ACTIVE TIME: **30 MINUTES**

TOTAL TIME: **2 HOURS**

Split Pea Soup with Smoked Ham

INGREDIENTS

2 tablespoons unsalted butter

1 onion, minced

1 carrot, peeled and minced

1 celery stalk, minced

5 cups chicken stock

1 cup split peas

½ lb. smoked ham, chopped

2 tablespoons finely chopped fresh parsley, plus more for garnish

1 bay leaf

1 teaspoon finely chopped fresh thyme

Salt and pepper, to taste

Lemon wedges, for serving

DIRECTIONS

1 Place the butter in a large saucepan and melt it over medium heat. Add the onion, carrot, and celery and cook, stirring frequently, until they have softened, about 5 minutes.

2 Add the stock, split peas, ham, parsley, bay leaf, and thyme. Bring the soup to a boil, reduce the heat to medium-low, and simmer, stirring occasionally, until the peas are al dente, about 1 hour.

3 Remove the bay leaf and discard it. Season the soup with salt and pepper and ladle it into warmed bowls. Garnish with additional parsley and serve with lemon wedges.

YIELD: **4 SERVINGS**

ACTIVE TIME: **30 MINUTES**

TOTAL TIME: **1 HOUR AND 30 MINUTES**

Mansaf

INGREDIENTS

2 tablespoons extra-virgin olive oil

1 onion, chopped

2 lbs. lamb shoulder, cubed

6 cups beef stock

Seeds from 2 cardamom pods

1 cup plain Greek yogurt

Salt and pepper, to taste

2 cups cooked long-grain rice

¼ cup pine nuts, toasted, for garnish

Fresh parsley, finely chopped, for garnish

DIRECTIONS

1 Place the olive oil in a saucepan and warm over medium-high heat. Add the onion and cook, stirring frequently, until it starts to soften, about 5 minutes. Add the lamb and cook until it is browned all over, about 8 minutes.

2 Add the stock and cardamom and bring the soup to a boil. Reduce the heat to medium-low, cover the pan, and simmer until the lamb is very tender, about 1 hour.

3 Stir in the yogurt, season with salt and pepper, and remove the soup from heat. Divide the rice between the serving bowls, ladle the soup over the rice, and garnish with the pine nuts and parsley.

Mansaf, see page 109

YIELD: **4 SERVINGS**

ACTIVE TIME: **20 MINUTES**

TOTAL TIME: **45 MINUTES**

Saffron & Mussel Soup

INGREDIENTS

3 lbs. mussels, rinsed well and debearded

3 cups white wine

4 tablespoons unsalted butter

2 leeks, trimmed, rinsed well, and chopped

2 celery stalks, chopped

¾ cup chopped fennel

1 carrot, peeled and minced

2 garlic cloves, minced

⅛ teaspoon saffron

2 cups heavy cream

Salt and pepper, to taste

3 tomatoes, chopped

Fresh parsley, finely chopped, for garnish

Microgreens, for garnish

Shaved radish, for garnish

Lemon wedges, for serving

DIRECTIONS

1 Place the mussels and the wine in a large saucepan, cover, and cook over medium heat, shaking the pan occasionally, for 4 to 5 minutes, until the majority of the mussels have opened.

2 Discard any unopened mussels. Drain, reserve the cooking liquid, and remove the meat from all but 18 of the mussels. Reserve the 18 mussels in their shells for garnish.

3 Add the butter to the saucepan and melt it over medium heat. Add the leeks, celery, fennel, carrot, and garlic and cook, stirring frequently, until the vegetables start to soften, about 5 minutes.

4 Strain the reserved liquid through a fine sieve and add it to the saucepan. Cook for 10 minutes, until the liquid has reduced by one-quarter.

5 Add the saffron and the cream and bring the soup to a boil. Reduce the heat to low, season with salt and pepper, add the mussels and tomatoes, and cook gently until heated through.

6 Ladle the soup into warmed bowls, garnish with the parsley, microgreens, radish, and reserved mussels, and serve with lemon wedges.

YIELD: **4 SERVINGS**

ACTIVE TIME: **20 MINUTES**

TOTAL TIME: **I HOUR AND I5 MINUTES**

Eggplant & Zucchini Soup

INGREDIENTS

1 large eggplant, peeled and chopped

2 large zucchini, chopped

1 onion, chopped

3 garlic cloves, minced

2 tablespoons extra-virgin olive oil

3 cups chicken or vegetable stock

1 tablespoon finely chopped fresh oregano

1 tablespoon chopped fresh mint, plus more for garnish

Salt and pepper, to taste

Tzatziki (see page 21), for serving

Pita Bread (see page 34), for serving

Minty Pickled Cucumbers (see page 49), for serving

DIRECTIONS

1   Preheat the oven to 425°F. Place the eggplant, zucchini, onion, and garlic in a baking dish, drizzle the olive oil over the mixture, and gently stir to coat. Place in the oven and roast for 30 minutes, removing to stir occasionally.

2   Remove from the oven and let the vegetables cool briefly.

3   Place half of the roasted vegetables in a food processor. Add the stock and blitz until pureed. Place the puree in a medium saucepan, add the remaining roasted vegetables, and bring to a boil.

4   Stir in the oregano and mint and season with salt and pepper. Cook for 2 minutes and ladle into warmed bowls. Garnish with additional mint and serve with the Tzatziki, Pita Bread, and Minty Pickled Cucumbers.

YIELD: **4 SERVINGS**

ACTIVE TIME: **20 MINUTES**

TOTAL TIME: **45 MINUTES**

Broccoli & Anchovy Soup

INGREDIENTS

1 tablespoon extra-virgin olive oil

1 tablespoon unsalted butter

1 onion, chopped

1 garlic clove, minced

1½ cups chopped portobello mushrooms

1 bird's eye chili pepper, stems and seeds removed, chopped

2 anchovies in olive oil, drained and minced

1 cup chopped tomatoes

¼ cup white wine

4 cups chicken or vegetable stock

2 cups broccoli florets

Salt and pepper, to taste

Parmesan cheese, freshly grated, for garnish

DIRECTIONS

1   Place the olive oil and butter in a saucepan and warm over low heat. When the butter has melted, add the onion, garlic, mushrooms, chili, and anchovies and cook, stirring frequently, until the onion starts to soften, about 5 minutes.

2   Stir in the tomatoes and the white wine and simmer, stirring occasionally, for 10 minutes.

3   Add the stock, raise the heat to medium-high, and bring the soup to a boil. Reduce the heat so that the soup simmers. Add the broccoli florets and cook for 10 minutes.

4   Season with salt and pepper, ladle into warmed bowls, and garnish with Parmesan cheese.

YIELD: **4 TO 6 SERVINGS**

ACTIVE TIME: **30 MINUTES**

TOTAL TIME: **1 HOUR**

Leek & Seafood Stew

DIRECTIONS

1 Place the olive oil in a medium saucepan and warm it over medium heat. Add the leeks, crushed coriander seeds, and red pepper flakes and cook, stirring occasionally, until the leeks start to soften, about 5 minutes.

2 Add the potatoes, tomatoes, stock, wine, bay leaves, star anise, orange zest, and saffron and bring the soup to a boil. Reduce the heat so that the soup simmers and cook until the potatoes are tender, about 15 minutes.

3 Add the cod and the squid to the soup and cook until cooked through, 3 to 4 minutes.

4 Add the shrimp and cook until they are cooked through, about 2 minutes. Season the soup with salt and pepper, ladle it into warmed bowls, and enjoy.

INGREDIENTS

2 tablespoons extra-virgin olive oil

White parts of 2 leeks, trimmed, rinsed well, and sliced thin

2 teaspoons coriander seeds, crushed

Pinch of red pepper flakes

3 cups multicolored little creamer potatoes, sliced thin

1 (14 oz.) can of diced tomatoes, with their liquid

4 cups fish stock

1 cup white wine

2 bay leaves

1 star anise pod

Zest of 1 orange

Pinch of saffron

1 lb. cod fillets, cut into ½-inch pieces

1 lb. small squid, bodies halved and scored, tentacles left whole

10 oz. shrimp, shelled and deveined

Salt and pepper, to taste

Romesco de Peix

DIRECTIONS

1   Place the almonds in a large cast-iron skillet and toast them over medium heat until they are just browned. Transfer them to a food processor and pulse until they are finely ground.

2   Place the saffron and boiling water in a bowl and let the mixture steep.

3   Place the olive oil in a Dutch oven and warm over medium heat. Add the onion and bell peppers and cook, stirring occasionally, until the peppers are tender, about 15 minutes.

4   Add the sweet paprika, smoked paprika, bay leaf, and tomato paste and cook, stirring constantly, for 1 minute. Add the sherry and bring the mixture to a boil. Boil for 5 minutes and then stir in the stock, tomatoes, saffron, and the soaking liquid. Stir to combine, season with salt and pepper, and reduce the heat so that the soup simmers.

5   Add the ground almonds and cook until the mixture thickens slightly, about 8 minutes. Add the fish and mussels, stir gently to incorporate, and simmer until the fish is cooked through and a majority of the mussels have opened, about 5 minutes. Discard any mussels that do not open.

6   Ladle the mixture into warmed bowls, garnish with cilantro, and enjoy.

INGREDIENTS

½ cup slivered almonds

½ teaspoon saffron

¼ cup boiling water

½ cup extra-virgin olive oil

1 large yellow onion, chopped

2 large red bell peppers, stems and seeds removed, chopped

2½ teaspoons sweet paprika

1 tablespoon smoked paprika

1 bay leaf

2 tablespoons tomato paste

½ cup sherry

2 cups fish stock

1 (28 oz.) can of chopped tomatoes, with their liquid

Salt and pepper, to taste

1½ lbs. monkfish fillets, chopped into large pieces

1 lb. mussels, rinsed well and debearded

Fresh cilantro, finely chopped, for garnish

YIELD: **12 SERVINGS**

ACTIVE TIME: **30 MINUTES**

TOTAL TIME: **2 HOURS**

Tunisian Butternut Squash Soup

INGREDIENTS

1 large butternut squash, halved and seeded

1 teaspoon Three-Pepper Harissa Sauce (see page 99)

1 teaspoon kosher salt

½ teaspoon black pepper

¼ cup fresh lemon juice

1 tablespoon lemon zest

1½ teaspoons lime zest

2 tablespoons extra-virgin olive oil

2 parsnips, peeled and cubed

2 tablespoons avocado oil

3 small shallots, diced

3 garlic cloves, sliced

8 cups chicken stock

DIRECTIONS

1   Preheat the oven to 400°F. Place the butternut squash on an aluminum foil–lined baking sheet, cut side up.

2   Place the harissa, salt, pepper, lemon juice, lemon zest, lime zest, and olive oil in a bowl and stir until combined.

3   Spread the mixture over the squash. Place the parsnips around the squash, drizzle the harissa mixture over them, and toss to coat.

4   Place the pan in the oven and roast until the squash and parsnips are fork-tender, about 1 hour. Remove from the oven and let the vegetables cool for 20 minutes.

5   Place the avocado oil in a large saucepan and warm it over medium heat. Add the shallots and cook, stirring frequently, until they are translucent, about 3 minutes.

6   Add the garlic and cook, stirring frequently, until fragrant, about 1 minute.

7   Scoop the squash's flesh into a food processor, add the parsnips and some of the stock, and puree until smooth.

8   Add the puree to the saucepan, add the remaining stock, and simmer until the flavor has developed to your liking, about 25 minutes.

9   Taste, adjust the seasoning as necessary, and ladle the soup into warmed bowls.

ENTREES

In the Mediterranean region, a main course satisfies without overwhelming, manages to comfort without also being so rich that the rest of the evening is unpleasant.

This increasingly rare approach is indebted to the incredible bounty that Mother Nature has made available in the area, a bit of good fortune that organically leads to a diet that is far more balanced than in other areas of the world, featuring copious amounts of vegetables, seafood as much if not more than the poultry that is ubiquitous on dinner tables in the Americas, and little, if any, beef.

YIELD: **6 SERVINGS**

ACTIVE TIME: **15 MINUTES**

TOTAL TIME: **30 MINUTES**

Whitefish Poached in Pepper Sauce

INGREDIENTS

2 lbs. whitefish (such as tilapia, halibut, or flounder)

3 tablespoons avocado oil

2 garlic cloves, sliced thin

2 medium onions, halved and sliced thin

1 red bell pepper, stem and seeds removed, sliced thin

1 orange bell pepper, stem and seeds removed, sliced thin

1 yellow bell pepper, stem and seeds removed, sliced thin

¼ teaspoon paprika

¼ teaspoon sea salt

Black pepper, to taste

½ teaspoon chili powder

1½ cups water

⅔ cup chopped fresh cilantro

DIRECTIONS

1 Cut the fish into 2 x 5-inch pieces and let them rest at room temperature.

2 Place the avocado oil in a large skillet and warm it over medium-low heat. Add the garlic and onions and cook, stirring occasionally, for 5 minutes. Add the peppers and cook for another 4 minutes.

3 Stir in the paprika, salt, black pepper, and chili powder. Add the water, raise the heat to medium-high, and bring to a boil.

4 Reduce the heat to low, place the fish slices on top of the vegetables, cover the pan, and cook for 5 minutes.

5 Use a fork to place some of the peppers and onions on top of the fish. Cover the pan and cook for another 5 minutes, or until the fish can easily be flaked with a fork. Taste the sauce and season as necessary.

6 Sprinkle the cilantro over the dish and enjoy.

YIELD: **8 SERVINGS**
ACTIVE TIME: **30 MINUTES**
TOTAL TIME: **2 HOURS AND 30 MINUTES**

Leg of Lamb with Garlic & Rosemary

INGREDIENTS

Extra-virgin olive oil, as needed

1 (7 lb.) semi-boneless leg of lamb

4 garlic cloves

1 tablespoon kosher salt, plus more to taste

2 tablespoons chopped fresh rosemary

2 tablespoons ras el hanout

2 tablespoons sumac

2 tablespoons berbere seasoning

½ teaspoon black pepper, plus more to taste

¼ cup dry red wine or beef stock

DIRECTIONS

1   Coat a roasting pan with olive oil and set it aside. Trim any fatty areas on the leg of lamb so that the fat is within approximately ¼ inch of the meat, keeping in mind that it is better to leave too much fat than too little. Pat the lamb dry and score the remaining fat with a sharp paring knife, making sure not to cut into the flesh.

2   Using a mortar and pestle, grind the garlic and salt into a paste. Add the rosemary, ras el hanout, sumac, berbere seasoning, and pepper and stir to combine.

3   Place the lamb in the roasting pan and rub the paste all over it. Let the lamb marinate at room temperature for 30 minutes.

4   Preheat the oven to 350°F and position a rack in the middle.

5   Place the lamb in the oven and roast until an instant-read thermometer inserted about 2 inches into the thickest part of the meat registers 130°F, about 1½ hours.

6   Remove the lamb from the oven, transfer it to a cutting board, and let it rest 15 to 25 minutes (the internal temperature will rise to about 135°F, perfect for medium-rare).

7   Place the wine or stock in the roasting pan and place it over high heat, scraping up any browned bits from the bottom of the pan. Season the pan sauce with salt and pepper and serve it beside the lamb.

Leg of Lamb with Garlic & Rosemary, see page 127

YIELD: **4 SERVINGS**

ACTIVE TIME: **20 MINUTES**

TOTAL TIME: **I HOUR AND 20 MINUTES**

Pomegranate & Honey–Glazed Chicken

INGREDIENTS

¼ cup avocado oil

1 large onion, chopped

3 garlic cloves, minced

½ cup pomegranate molasses

½ cup sweetened pomegranate juice

½ cup honey

2 cups chicken stock

1 teaspoon cumin

½ teaspoon ground ginger

⅛ teaspoon allspice

½ teaspoon turmeric

4 lbs. bone-in, skin-on chicken pieces

Salt and pepper, to taste

Pomegranate seeds, for garnish

DIRECTIONS

1　Place 2 tablespoons of the avocado oil in a large skillet and warm it over medium-high heat. Add the onion and cook, stirring occasionally, until it is soft and translucent, about 3 minutes.

2　Add the garlic and cook, stirring frequently, until fragrant, about 1 minute. Stir in the pomegranate molasses, pomegranate juice, honey, stock, and seasonings and bring the mixture to a boil. Lower the heat and simmer the sauce until it has reduced by half and thickened slightly, about 20 minutes. Taste the sauce and adjust the seasoning as necessary. Transfer the sauce to a bowl and set it aside.

3　Rinse the chicken pieces, pat them dry, and season with salt and pepper.

4　Place the remaining avocado oil in the pan. Add the chicken pieces, skin side down, and cook until browned. Turn the chicken over, pour the sauce into the pan, reduce the heat, and cover the pan. Cook the chicken until cooked through and tender, 35 to 40 minutes.

5　Transfer the cooked chicken to a platter, garnish with pomegranate seeds, and enjoy.

Sumac Chicken & Rice

INGREDIENTS

¼ cup sumac

Zest of 1 lemon

1½ teaspoons kosher salt

¼ teaspoon white pepper

6 bone-in, skin-on chicken legs

3 cups basmati or jasmine rice, rinsed and drained

½ cup pine nuts

3 tablespoons berberis, dried cranberries, or cherries

1 teaspoon turmeric

2 tablespoons avocado oil, plus more to taste

1 red onion, halved and sliced

1 lemon, sliced thin

1½ cups chicken stock

DIRECTIONS

1   Preheat the oven to 400°F and position a rack in the middle. Place the sumac, lemon zest, 1 teaspoon of the salt, and white pepper in a small bowl and stir to combine.

2   Rub the spice mixture under the skin and on top of the chicken.

3   In a roasting pan, combine the rice, pine nuts, berberis, turmeric, remaining salt, and avocado oil until the rice is a beautiful yellow color. Press the rice down so that it's in an even layer.

4   Top the rice with the slices of red onion and lay the chicken on top of the onion. Top each piece of chicken with a lemon slice.

5   Pour the stock around the chicken, onto the rice. Drizzle the chicken with a generous amount of avocado oil.

6   Cover the roasting pan tightly with aluminum foil and place it in the oven. Roast the chicken for 40 minutes. Remove the foil and roast until the chicken is cooked through and the rice has soaked up all of the liquid, 20 to 25 minutes. Remove from the oven and enjoy.

YIELD: **2 SERVINGS**

ACTIVE TIME: **15 MINUTES**

TOTAL TIME: **2 HOURS AND 15 MINUTES**

Olive Oil–Poached Fluke

INGREDIENTS

½ lb. fluke fillet

1¼ cups extra-virgin olive oil

1 teaspoon kosher salt

Pinch of black pepper

½ lemon

Fresh parsley, for garnish

DIRECTIONS

1 Place the fluke and 1 cup of the olive oil in a vacuum bag and vacuum-seal it. Cook it sous vide at 145°F for 1 hour.

2 Remove the fluke from the water bath, place it in the refrigerator, and chill for 1 hour.

3 Slice the fish into 1-inch-thick pieces and arrange them on chilled serving plates. Season with the salt and pepper, drizzle the remaining olive oil around the plate, and squeeze the lemon over the pieces of fluke. Garnish with parsley and enjoy.

Olive Oil–Poached Fluke, see page 133

YIELD: **2 SERVINGS**

ACTIVE TIME: **25 MINUTES**

TOTAL TIME: **3 HOURS**

Sumac & Lime Mahimahi

INGREDIENTS

Juice of 2 limes

1 tablespoon sumac

1 teaspoon honey

1 teaspoon kosher salt

1 garlic clove, minced

2 (6 oz.) mahimahi fillets

1 tablespoon extra-virgin olive oil

Couscous, cooked, for serving

DIRECTIONS

1   In a small bowl, whisk together the lime juice, sumac, honey, salt, and garlic. Add the mahimahi and stir until the fillets are coated. Chill in the refrigerator for 2 hours.

2   Place the olive oil in a skillet and warm it over medium heat. Add the mahimahi to the pan and cook until it is browned on both sides and flakes easily at the touch of a fork, 8 to 10 minutes.

3   Remove the mahimahi from the pan and serve over couscous.

YIELD: **2 SERVINGS**
ACTIVE TIME: **20 MINUTES**
TOTAL TIME: **40 MINUTES**

Whole Branzino

INGREDIENTS

1 to 2 lb. whole branzino

2 fresh basil leaves

1 tablespoon kosher salt

1 tablespoon black pepper

2 tablespoons extra-virgin olive oil

½ lemon

DIRECTIONS

1   Preheat the oven to 425°F. Clean the fish, remove the bones, and descale it. Pat it dry with paper towels and rub the inside of the fish with the basil leaves. Season it with the salt and pepper and close the fish back up.

2   Place the olive oil in a large cast-iron skillet and warm it over high heat. Place the fish in the pan and cook until it is browned on both sides, 8 to 10 minutes, turning it as little as possible.

3   Place the pan in the oven and roast the fish until the internal temperature is 145°F, about 10 minutes.

4   Remove from the oven and transfer the branzino to a large platter. Squeeze the lemon over the top and enjoy.

Whole Branzino, see page 137

YIELD: **4 SERVINGS**
ACTIVE TIME: **30 MINUTES**
TOTAL TIME: **1 HOUR**

Shakshuka

INGREDIENTS

2 tablespoons extra-virgin olive oil

1 onion, chopped

2 green bell peppers, stems and seeds removed, chopped

2 garlic cloves, minced

1 teaspoon coriander

1 teaspoon sweet paprika

½ teaspoon cumin

1 teaspoon turmeric

Pinch of red pepper flakes

2 tablespoons tomato paste

5 ripe tomatoes, chopped

Salt and pepper, to taste

6 eggs

1 cup crumbled feta cheese

¼ cup chopped fresh parsley, for garnish

¼ cup chopped fresh mint, for garnish

DIRECTIONS

1 Place the olive oil in a large cast-iron skillet and warm it over medium heat. Add the onion and cook, stirring occasionally, until it has softened, about 5 minutes. Add the bell peppers and cook, stirring occasionally, until they have softened, about 5 minutes.

2 Add the garlic, coriander, paprika, cumin, turmeric, red pepper flakes, and tomato paste and cook, stirring continually, for 1 minute. Add the tomatoes and bring the mixture to a boil. Reduce the heat, cover the pan, and simmer for 15 minutes.

3 Remove the cover and cook until the shakshuka has reduced slightly, about 5 minutes.

4 Season the shakshuka with salt and pepper. Using the back of a wooden spoon, make six wells in the mixture. Crack an egg into each well and sprinkle the feta over the dish.

5 Reduce the heat to a simmer, cover the pan, and cook until the egg whites are set, 6 to 8 minutes.

6 Remove the pan from heat, garnish with parsley and mint, and enjoy.

YIELD: **4 SERVINGS**
ACTIVE TIME: **45 MINUTES**
TOTAL TIME: **5 HOURS**

Sweet & Sour Short Ribs

INGREDIENTS

Rack of short ribs
(3- to 4-bone)

2 tablespoons kosher salt

3 tablespoons black pepper

¼ cup extra-virgin olive oil

1 onion, quartered

8 garlic cloves, minced

2 apples, peeled and sliced

1 tablespoon sumac

½ cup white vinegar

¼ cup honey

DIRECTIONS

1 Preheat the oven to 300°F. Using a sharp knife, remove the silver skin, connective tissue, and any excess fat from the rack of ribs.

2 In a small bowl, combine the salt and pepper. Rub the mixture over the short ribs.

3 Warm a roasting pan or a very large skillet over high heat. After 5 minutes or so add a tablespoon of the olive oil and the short ribs to the pan. Cook until they are browned all over, about 10 minutes. Remove the ribs from the pan and set them in a large baking dish or roasting pan. Keep the pan over the high heat.

4 Add the onion, garlic, apples, remaining olive oil, and sumac to the pan and cook, stirring continuously, for 1 minute.

5 Pour the mixture over the ribs and then drizzle the vinegar and honey over them. Cover the pan with foil, place the pan in the oven, and braise for 4 hours.

6 Remove the pan from the oven and check the ribs. If the meat is very tender, to where it is just about to fall off the bone, cut the ribs between the bones. If not, return the pan to the oven and continue to braise the ribs until tender, checking every 30 minutes or so.

7 To serve, spoon some of the pan juices, apples, and onions over the ribs.

YIELD: **4 SERVINGS**
ACTIVE TIME: **30 MINUTES**
TOTAL TIME: **2 HOURS AND 30 MINUTES**

Risi e Bisi

INGREDIENTS

2 tablespoons extra-virgin olive oil

6 oz. thinly sliced prosciutto, cut into ¼-inch-wide strips

2 shallots, minced

1 garlic cloves, minced

1 cup Arborio rice

½ cup white wine

Chicken stock, warmed, as needed

1 lb. frozen peas

1 cup freshly grated Parmesan cheese

Juice of ½ lemon

Salt and pepper, to taste

Fresh parsley, chopped, for garnish

DIRECTIONS

1   Place the olive oil in a large saucepan and warm it over medium-high heat. Add the prosciutto and cook, stirring frequently, until it is golden brown and crispy, about 5 minutes. Using a slotted spoon, transfer the prosciutto to a paper towel–lined plate and let it drain.

2   Add the shallots to the saucepan and cook, stirring occasionally, until they start to soften, about 3 minutes.

3   Add the garlic and rice and cook, stirring frequently, for 2 minutes.

4   Add the white wine and cook, stirring frequently, until the rice has absorbed the wine.

5   While stirring continually, add the stock ¼ cup at a time, waiting until each addition has been fully absorbed before adding more. Add stock until the rice is tender, about 15 minutes.

6   Add the frozen peas and cook, stirring frequently, until warmed through, 4 to 5 minutes.

7   Stir in the Parmesan and lemon juice. Season the dish with salt and pepper, garnish with the crispy prosciutto and parsley, and enjoy.

YIELD: **6 SERVINGS**
ACTIVE TIME: **30 MINUTES**
TOTAL TIME: **1 HOUR**

Ratatouille with Poached Eggs

INGREDIENTS

¼ cup extra-virgin olive oil

1 cup chopped onion

4 garlic cloves, minced

2 tablespoons tomato paste

1 cup chopped red
bell pepper

1 cup chopped yellow
bell pepper

1 cup chopped zucchini

½ cup water

2 tablespoons herbes
de Provence

Salt and pepper, to taste

6 eggs

¼ cup fresh basil leaves

½ cup shaved
Parmesan cheese

DIRECTIONS

1   Place the olive oil in a Dutch oven and warm it over medium heat. Add the onion and cook, stirring occasionally, until it has softened, about 5 minutes. Add the garlic and tomato paste and cook, stirring continually, for 1 minute.

2   Add the bell peppers and cook, stirring occasionally, until they have softened, about 5 minutes.

3   Add the zucchini, water, and herbes de Provence, cover the pot, and cook for 10 minutes. Remove the cover and cook until the liquid has reduced, about 5 minutes.

4   Season the ratatouille with salt and pepper. Using the back of a wooden spoon, make six wells in the ratatouille. Gently crack an egg into each well, reduce the heat so that the ratatouille simmers, and cover the pot. Cook until the egg whites are set, 6 to 8 minutes.

5   Spoon the ratatouille and poached eggs into bowls, garnish each portion with basil and Parmesan, and enjoy.

YIELD: **4 TO 6 SERVINGS**

ACTIVE TIME: **30 MINUTES**

TOTAL TIME: **I HOUR AND 30 MINUTES**

Easy Paella

DIRECTIONS

1 Preheat the oven to 350°F. Place the olive oil in a Dutch oven and warm it over medium-high heat. Add the chicken and cook until browned all over, about 6 minutes, stirring as necessary. Remove the chicken thighs with a slotted spoon and place them in a bowl.

2 Add the chorizo to the pot and cook, stirring occasionally, until it is browned all over, about 6 minutes, breaking it up with a wooden spoon. Transfer to the bowl with the chicken.

3 Add the onion to the pot and cook, stirring occasionally, until it has softened, about 5 minutes. Add the bell pepper and cook, stirring occasionally, for 3 minutes.

4 Add the garlic and cook, stirring frequently, for 1 minute. Stir in the tomatoes and cook until the mixture thickens slightly, about 3 minutes. Add the rice and cook for 2 minutes.

5 Stir in the stock, wine, saffron, paprika, and bay leaves and bring the mixture to a boil, stirring frequently. Return the chicken and chorizo to the pot, season the mixture with salt and pepper, cover the pot, and place it in the oven.

6 Bake until all the liquid has evaporated, about 15 minutes, stirring occasionally.

7 Remove the pot from the oven and place the mussels and shrimp on top of the rice. Make sure to put the mussels in with their hinge down. Cover the pot and return it to the oven. Bake until the shrimp is cooked through and the majority of the mussels have opened, about 10 minutes.

8 Remove the paella from the oven, discard the bay leaves and any mussels that did not open, and garnish with parsley. Serve with lemon wedges and enjoy.

INGREDIENTS

2 tablespoons extra-virgin olive oil

1½ lbs. boneless, skinless chicken thighs, chopped into 1-inch cubes

9 oz. ground chorizo

1 onion, chopped

1 red bell pepper, stem and seeds removed, chopped

6 garlic cloves, minced

1 (14 oz.) can of diced tomatoes, drained

2 cups bomba rice

4 cups chicken stock

⅓ cup white wine

½ teaspoon saffron

1 teaspoon paprika

2 bay leaves

Salt and pepper, to taste

16 mussels, scrubbed and debearded

1 lb. jumbo shrimp, shells removed, deveined

¾ cup frozen peas

Fresh parsley, chopped, for garnish

Lemon wedges, for serving

YIELD: **4 SERVINGS**
ACTIVE TIME: **10 MINUTES**
TOTAL TIME: **20 MINUTES**

Garlic & Lime Calamari

INGREDIENTS

1½ lbs. calamari, sliced
into rings

2 tablespoons extra-virgin
olive oil

1 tablespoon unsalted butter

10 garlic cloves, chopped

3 tablespoons white wine

Juice of 1½ limes

Salt and pepper, to taste

Pinch of cayenne pepper

3 tablespoons chopped
fresh dill

DIRECTIONS

1 Pat the calamari dry and set it aside. Place the olive oil and butter in a large cast-iron skillet and warm over medium-high heat. When the butter starts to foam, add the garlic and cook, stirring continuously, until fragrant, about 1 minute.

2 Add the calamari to the pan, cook for 2 minutes, and then stir in the wine and lime juice. Cook for another 30 seconds, until warmed through, and remove the pan from heat.

3 Season with salt and pepper, stir in the cayenne and dill, and enjoy.

YIELD: **4 TO 6 SERVINGS**
ACTIVE TIME: **20 MINUTES**
TOTAL TIME: **I HOUR**

Spaghetti al Tonno

INGREDIENTS

2 tablespoons avocado oil

3 garlic cloves, minced

1 small yellow onion, minced

⅛ teaspoon red pepper flakes

3 cups tomato passata
(strained tomatoes)

Salt and pepper, to taste

1 lb. spaghetti

6 oz. tuna in olive oil, drained

4 sprigs of fresh parsley,
chopped

DIRECTIONS

1 Place the avocado oil in a medium saucepan and
   warm it over medium-low heat. Add the garlic and
   onion and cook, stirring frequently, until the onion
   just starts to soften, about 5 minutes.

2 Add the red pepper flakes and passata, season with
   salt and pepper, and stir until well combined.

3 Add about 2 cups of water to the sauce and bring it
   to a boil. Cover the pan, reduce the heat to medium-
   low, and cook until the sauce has thickened, about
   45 minutes.

4 While the sauce is simmering, bring a large pot of
   water to a boil.

5 Salt the water, add the pasta, and cook until al dente,
   6 to 8 minutes.

6 Add the drained tuna to the tomato sauce and
   continue to simmer for about 5 minutes.

7 Drain the pasta and toss it with some of the tomato
   sauce. To serve, top each portion of pasta with more
   sauce and some of the parsley.

Spaghetti al Tonno, see page 151

YIELD: **4 SERVINGS**

ACTIVE TIME: **30 MINUTES**

TOTAL TIME: **1 HOUR AND 20 MINUTES**

Stuffed Eggplants

INGREDIENTS

2 large eggplants, halved

2 tablespoons extra-virgin olive oil, plus more as needed

½ cup quinoa

1 cup water

2 onions, chopped

3 garlic cloves, minced

2 bell peppers, stems and seeds removed, chopped

1 lb. ground lamb

Salt and pepper, to taste

½ teaspoon garam masala

2 teaspoons cumin

Fresh parsley, finely chopped, for garnish

DIRECTIONS

1   Preheat the oven to 400°F. Place the eggplants on a baking sheet, drizzle olive oil over the top, and place them in the oven. Roast until the flesh is tender, about 30 minutes. Remove from the oven and let the eggplants cool slightly. When cool enough to handle, scoop out the flesh, mince it, and place it in a mixing bowl. Set the hollowed-out eggplants aside and leave the oven on.

2   Place the quinoa and water in a saucepan and bring to a boil over medium heat. Let the quinoa boil until it has absorbed all of the water. Remove the pan from heat, cover it, and let it steam for 5 minutes. Fluff with a fork and let cool slightly.

3   Place the olive oil in a large skillet and warm it over medium-high heat. When the oil starts to shimmer, add the onions, garlic, and bell peppers and cook, stirring frequently, until the onions and peppers start to soften, about 5 minutes. Add the lamb, season it with salt and pepper, stir in the garam masala and cumin, and cook, breaking the lamb up with a fork, until it is browned, about 6 minutes. Transfer the mixture to the bowl containing the minced eggplant, while adding the quinoa to the bowl at the same time, and stir until the mixture is combined.

4   Fill the cavities of the hollowed-out eggplants with the lamb-and-quinoa mixture. Place the eggplants on a baking sheet, place them in the oven, and roast until they are starting to collapse, about 15 minutes. Remove from the oven and let the stuffed eggplants cool slightly before garnishing with the parsley and serving.

YIELD: **6 SERVINGS**

ACTIVE TIME: **30 MINUTES**

TOTAL TIME: **2 HOURS**

Cedar-Plank Salmon

INGREDIENTS

2 tablespoons grainy mustard

2 tablespoons mild honey or pure maple syrup

1 teaspoon finely chopped fresh rosemary

1 tablespoon lemon zest

½ teaspoon kosher salt

½ teaspoon black pepper

2 lb. skin-on salmon fillet (about 1½ inches thick)

DIRECTIONS

1 Submerge a cedar grilling plank in water for 2 hours.

2 Prepare a gas or charcoal grill for medium-high heat (450°F).

3 In a bowl, combine the mustard, honey, rosemary, lemon zest, salt, and pepper and stir until well combined. Spread the mixture on the flesh of the salmon and let it stand at room temperature for 15 minutes.

4 Place the salmon on the plank, skin side down. Grill until the salmon is just cooked through and the edges are browned, 13 to 15 minutes.

5 Remove the salmon from the grill and let it rest on the plank for 3 minutes before enjoying.

YIELD: **8 SERVINGS**
ACTIVE TIME: **20 MINUTES**
TOTAL TIME: **45 MINUTES**

Chermoula Sea Bass

INGREDIENTS

8 Mediterranean sea bass fillets, skin removed

3 tablespoons Chermoula Sauce (see page 89)

Lemon wedges, for serving

DIRECTIONS

1 Preheat the oven to 425°F. Rub the sea bass with the chermoula. Place a 2-inch sheet of parchment paper on a work surface and fold it in half lengthwise.

2 Arrange four of the fillets along one edge of the seam. Fold the parchment over the fillets and fold in the edges to make a pouch. Repeat with a second sheet of parchment and the remaining fillets.

3 Carefully transfer the pouches to a rimmed baking sheet. Place the pan in the oven and bake until the fish is cooked through and flakes easily at the touch of a fork, 10 to 12 minutes.

4 Remove from the oven and carefully open the pouches; be careful of the steam that escapes. Serve the sea bass immediately with the lemon wedges.

DESSERTS

The health and wellness industry's appropriation of the concept of Mediterranean cuisine tends to make people think there's not all that much going on in terms of sweets in the region. And, once again, those assumptions carry folks astray. First off, there's baklava, which stands beside pizza and fried chicken as the rare item that there is no bad version of, only varying levels of great. Second, the exceptional produce in the area (figs, lemons, honey, to name a few) leads to a predilection for confections that can satisfy without leading one awry in their quest to live a healthier life.

Baklava

DIRECTIONS

1 Place 1 cup of the sugar, the water, honey, cinnamon stick, whole cloves, and half of the sea salt in a saucepan and bring the mixture to a boil, stirring to dissolve the sugar. Reduce the heat and simmer until the mixture is syrupy, about 5 minutes. Remove the pan from heat and let the syrup cool. When it is cool, strain the syrup and set it aside.

2 Place the almonds in a food processor and pulse until finely chopped. Place the almonds in a bowl, add the walnuts to the food processor, and pulse and they are finely chopped. Add them to the bowl along with the cinnamon, ground cloves, and remaining sugar and salt and stir until combined. Set the mixture aside.

3 Preheat the oven to 300°F. Line a 10 x 8-inch baking pan with parchment paper. Place one sheet of phyllo in the pan and keep the remaining phyllo covered. Brush the sheet with some of the melted butter and place another sheet of phyllo on top. Repeat this four more times, so that you have a layer of 10 buttered phyllo sheets.

4 Spread 1 cup of the nut mixture over the layer of phyllo. Top this with another layer of 10 buttered phyllo sheets, spread another cup of the nut mixture over it, and repeat.

5 Top the baklava with another layer of 10 buttered phyllo sheets. Using a serrated knife, cut the baklava into diamonds, making sure not to cut all the way through the bottom layer. Place the baklava in the oven and bake until it is golden brown, about 45 minutes, rotating the pan halfway through.

6 Remove the baklava from the oven and pour the syrup over it. Let the baklava cool completely, cut it all the way through, and enjoy.

INGREDIENTS

1 cup plus 2 tablespoons sugar

¾ cup water

½ cup honey

1 cinnamon stick

5 whole cloves

¼ teaspoon fine sea salt

1½ cups slivered almonds

1½ cups walnuts

1 teaspoon cinnamon

¼ teaspoon ground cloves

1 lb. phyllo dough, thawed

1 cup unsalted butter, melted

YIELD: **4 SERVINGS**

ACTIVE TIME: **30 MINUTES**

TOTAL TIME: **2 HOURS**

Zeppole

INGREDIENTS

1½ cups all-purpose flour

1 tablespoon plus 1 teaspoon baking powder

¼ teaspoon fine sea salt

2 eggs

2 tablespoons sugar

2 cups ricotta cheese

Zest of 1 orange

1 cup milk

1 teaspoon pure vanilla extract

Canola oil, as needed

¼ cup confectioners' sugar

DIRECTIONS

1 Sift the flour, baking powder, and salt into a bowl. Set the mixture aside.

2 Place the eggs and sugar in a separate bowl and whisk to combine. Add the ricotta, whisk to incorporate, and then stir in the orange zest, milk, and vanilla.

3 Gradually incorporate the dry mixture until it comes together as a smooth batter. Place the batter in the refrigerator and chill for 1 hour.

4 Add canola oil to a Dutch oven until it is about 2 inches deep and warm it to 350°F. Drop tablespoons of the batter into the hot oil, taking care not to crowd the pot, and fry until the zeppole are golden brown. Transfer the fried zeppole to a paper towel–lined plate and dust them with confectioners' sugar. Enjoy at room temperature.

Pasteli

INGREDIENTS

2 cups sesame seeds

1 cup honey

½ teaspoon kosher salt

1 teaspoon pure
vanilla extract

DIRECTIONS

1   Preheat the oven to 350°F. Line a square 8-inch baking pan with parchment paper. Place the sesame seeds on a baking sheet, place them in the oven, and toast until golden brown, about 5 minutes. Remove from the oven and let the sesame seeds cool.

2   Place the honey in a small saucepan and warm it over medium-high heat. Boil the honey until it reaches 310°F.

3   Remove the pan from heat, stir in the salt, vanilla, and toasted sesame seeds, and pour the mixture into the baking pan. Let the mixture cool for 15 minutes.

4   Cut the bars into the desired shape; they should still be warm. Enjoy immediately or at room temperature.

YIELD: **20 SUFGANIYOT**
ACTIVE TIME: **45 MINUTES**
TOTAL TIME: **3 HOURS**

Sufganiyot

INGREDIENTS

3½ tablespoons unsalted butter, chopped, plus more as needed

3½ cups all-purpose flour, plus more as needed

½ teaspoon fine sea salt

¼ cup sugar

1 tablespoon instant yeast

1 egg

1¼ cups lukewarm milk (85°F)

Avocado oil, as needed

½ cup strawberry or raspberry jam

¼ cup confectioners' sugar

DIRECTIONS

1 Coat a mixing bowl with some butter and set it aside. Sift the flour into the work bowl of a stand mixer fitted with the dough hook. Add the salt, sugar, and yeast and stir to incorporate.

2 Add the egg and butter to the mixture and mix to incorporate. Gradually add the milk and work the mixture until it comes together as a soft dough, 8 to 10 minutes.

3 Form the dough into a ball and place it in the buttered mixing bowl. Cover with a linen towel and let it rise until doubled in size, about 2 hours.

4 Line two baking sheets with parchment paper. Place the dough on a flour-dusted work surface and roll it out until it is about ¾ inch thick. Cut the dough into 2-inch circles, place them on the baking sheets, and cover with a linen towel. Let them rise for another 20 minutes.

5 Add avocado oil to a Dutch oven until it is about 2 inches deep and warm it to 325°F. Add the dough in batches of 4 and fry until golden brown, about 6 minutes, turning them over halfway through.

6 Drain the sufganiyot on a paper towel–lined plate. Fill a piping bag with the jam, and make a small slit on the top of each sufganiyah. Place the piping bag in the slit and fill until you see the filling coming back out. Sprinkle with confectioners' sugar and enjoy.

YIELD: **12 SERVINGS**

ACTIVE TIME: **20 MINUTES**

TOTAL TIME: **36 HOURS**

Classic Halvah

INGREDIENTS

1½ cups tahini paste, stirred well

2 cups honey

2 cups sliced almonds, toasted

DIRECTIONS

1 Coat a loaf pan with nonstick cooking spray. Place the tahini in a small saucepan.

2 Place the honey in a saucepan fitted with a candy thermometer and warm it over medium heat until it reaches 240°F. Remove the pan from heat.

3 Warm the tahini to 120°F.

4 Add the warmed tahini to the honey and stir the mixture with a wooden spoon. It will look broken at first, but after a few minutes the mixture will come together smoothly.

5 Add the nuts and continue to stir the mixture until it starts to stiffen, 6 to 8 minutes.

6 Pour the mixture into the loaf pan and let it cool to room temperature.

7 Cover the pan tightly with plastic wrap and refrigerate for 36 hours. This will allow sugar crystals to form, which will give the halvah its distinctive texture.

8 Invert the halvah to remove it from the pan and use a sharp knife to cut it into the desired portions.

Goat Cheese & Honey Panna Cotta

INGREDIENTS

2 tablespoons water

1 envelope of unflavored gelatin

2½ cups heavy cream

4 oz. creamy goat cheese

½ cup honey, plus more for garnish

Fresh berries, for garnish

DIRECTIONS

1   Place the water in a small saucepan and warm it over medium heat. Sprinkle the gelatin over the water and stir until thoroughly combined. The mixture will very quickly become a paste—remove the pan from heat as soon as it does and set it aside.

2   Place the cream in another small saucepan and warm it over medium heat. Stir in the goat cheese and cook until it has dissolved. Add the honey and cook until it has been incorporated.

3   Place the gelatin over low heat and gradually add the cream mixture, stirring continually. When all of the cream mixture has been incorporated, raise the heat to medium and cook the mixture until it has thickened, about 10 minutes, stirring frequently.

4   Remove the pan from heat and pour the mixture into 4-oz. ramekins or mason jars. Place them in the refrigerator and chill until they have set, 4 to 5 hours.

5   To serve, garnish each portion with fresh berries and honey.

YIELD: **6 SERVINGS**

ACTIVE TIME: **30 MINUTES**

TOTAL TIME: **4 HOURS AND 30 MINUTES**

Classic Malabi

INGREDIENTS

For the Pudding

4 cups milk

⅔ cup cornstarch

1 teaspoon rose water

1 cup heavy cream

½ cup sugar

½ cup roasted peanuts or pistachios, for garnish

Shredded coconut, for garnish

For the Syrup

½ cup water

½ cup sugar

1 teaspoon rose water

2 to 3 drops of red food coloring

DIRECTIONS

1   To begin preparations for the pudding, place 1 cup of the milk in a bowl, add the cornstarch and rose water, and stir until the mixture is smooth. Set aside.

2   Place the remaining milk, heavy cream, and sugar in a saucepan. Bring to a simmer, stirring constantly, reduce the heat to low, and stir in the cornstarch mixture.

3   Cook, stirring constantly, until the mixture starts to thicken, 3 to 4 minutes. Pour the pudding into ramekins or small mason jars, place plastic wrap directly on the surface to prevent a skin from forming, and let the pudding cool completely. When it has cooled, chill in the refrigerator for 4 hours.

4   To prepare the syrup, place the water, sugar, and rose water in a saucepan and bring to a boil, stirring to dissolve the sugar. Stir in the food coloring, boil for another 2 minutes, and remove the pan from heat. Let the syrup cool completely.

5   When the malabi has chilled for 4 hours, pour 1 to 2 tablespoons of the syrup over each portion, and garnish with peanuts or pistachios and shredded coconut.

Classic Malabi, see page 173

Spiced Honey Cake

INGREDIENTS

2 cups gluten-free
all-purpose baking flour

1½ teaspoons baking powder

½ teaspoon baking soda

½ teaspoon sea salt

1½ teaspoons cinnamon

½ teaspoon ground ginger

⅛ teaspoon freshly
grated nutmeg

⅔ cup sugar

¼ cup packed light
brown sugar

½ cup avocado oil

½ cup honey

1 large egg

1 large egg yolk

Seeds from ½ vanilla bean

½ cup fresh orange juice

½ cup buttermilk

DIRECTIONS

1   Preheat the oven to 350°F. Coat a 9-inch cake pan with nonstick cooking spray and line the bottom with a circle of parchment paper.

2   Place the flour, baking powder, baking soda, salt, cinnamon, ginger, and nutmeg in a mixing bowl and stir to combine.

3   Combine the sugar, brown sugar, avocado oil, honey, egg, and egg yolk in the work bowl of a stand mixer fitted with the paddle attachment. Add the vanilla seeds and beat the mixture until it is pale and thick, about 4 minutes. Reduce the speed to medium-low and gradually pour in the orange juice and buttermilk. Beat until frothy, about 2 minutes. Reduce speed to low and gradually incorporate the dry mixture. Beat until the mixture comes together as a thin, pancake-like batter.

4   Pour the batter into the prepared pan and bake until the cake is golden brown and the center springs back when gently pressed (a cake tester inserted will not come out clean), 45 to 55 minutes.

5   Remove the cake from the oven, place the pan on a wire rack, and let the cake cool for 20 minutes. Run a knife around the edge of the cake to loosen it and invert it onto the rack. Let the cake cool completely before enjoying.

YIELD: **15 SERVINGS**
ACTIVE TIME: **40 MINUTES**
TOTAL TIME: **3 HOURS**

Sfenj

INGREDIENTS

4 cups all-purpose flour

2 teaspoons instant yeast

1 teaspoon fine sea salt

1 tablespoon sugar

2 large egg yolks

1½ cups lukewarm water (90°F)

Avocado oil, as needed

Confectioners' sugar or honey, for topping

DIRECTIONS

1   Place the flour, yeast, salt, and sugar in a mixing bowl and stir to combine. Add the egg yolks and slowly drizzle in the water while mixing by hand.

2   Knead the mixture until it comes together as a sticky, smooth, and soft dough.

3   Spray the dough with nonstick cooking spray and cover the bowl with plastic wrap. Let the dough rise at room temperature for 2 hours.

4   Coat a large baking sheet with some avocado oil. Set it aside.

5   Divide the dough into 15 parts, roll each piece into a ball, and place it on the greased baking sheet. Cover the balls of dough with a slightly damp linen towel and let them rise for another 30 minutes.

6   Add avocado oil to a large, deep skillet until it is one-third to halfway full and warm it to 375°F.

7   Using your forefinger and thumb, make a hole in the center of each dough ball and gently slip them into the hot oil. Fry until lightly golden brown all over, turning the sfenj as necessary.

8   Top the fried sfenj with confectioners' sugar or honey and enjoy immediately.

Sfenj, see page 177

YIELD: **4 SERVINGS**
ACTIVE TIME: **20 MINUTES**
TOTAL TIME: **I HOUR AND 20 MINUTES**

Sumac, Spelt & Apple Cake

INGREDIENTS

For the Applesauce

2 large granny smith apples, peeled, cored, and chopped

1 tablespoon fresh lemon juice

½ cup water

For the Cake

1⅔ cups spelt flour

½ cup ground almonds

1 tablespoon sumac, plus more for topping

1 teaspoon baking powder

1 teaspoon baking soda

¼ cup avocado oil

½ cup plus 2 tablespoons sugar

3 golden apples, peeled, cored, and finely diced

½ cup confectioners' sugar, plus more as needed

1 tablespoon fresh lemon juice, plus more as needed

DIRECTIONS

1 To prepare the applesauce, place all of the ingredients in a saucepan and bring to a simmer. Cook until the apples are completely tender, 10 to 12 minutes. Remove the pan from heat and mash the apples until smooth. Set the applesauce aside.

2 Preheat the oven to 350°F. Coat a 1-pound loaf pan with cooking spray and line it with parchment paper. To begin preparations for the cake, place the flour, ground almonds, sumac, baking powder and baking soda in a mixing bowl and stir to combine.

3 Place the avocado oil, sugar, and 1½ cups of the applesauce in a separate bowl and stir to combine. Add the wet mixture to the dry mixture and gently stir until the mixture comes together as a thick batter, making sure there are no clumps of flour. Stir in the apples.

4 Pour the batter into the loaf pan, place it in the oven, and bake until a cake tester inserted into the center of the cake comes out clean, 45 to 50 minutes.

5 Remove the cake from the oven and let it cool completely in the pan.

6 Place the confectioners' sugar and lemon juice in a mixing bowl and whisk the mixture until it is thick enough to coat the back of a wooden spoon. If it's too thin, add more sugar; if too thick, add more lemon juice.

7 Drizzle the icing over the cake, top with additional sumac, and enjoy.

Debla

INGREDIENTS

5 large eggs, beaten

1 teaspoon baking soda

3 cups all-purpose flour

Avocado oil, as needed

2 cups sugar

⅛ teaspoon fresh lemon juice

⅛ teaspoon orange blossom water

⅛ teaspoon rose water

⅛ teaspoon pure vanilla extract

DIRECTIONS

1   Place the eggs, baking soda, and 2½ cups of the flour in a mixing bowl and work the mixture until it comes together as a dough. Divide the dough into five pieces. Roll out each piece until it is paper thin.

2   Add avocado oil to a deep skillet until it is 1 inch deep and warm it to 325°F. Cut the dough into strips that are 2 inches wide and about 12 inches long. Prick the strips all over with a fork. Wrap a strip around one prong of a wide fork and fry it, coiling the dough around itself as it fries until it is lightly browned all over. Transfer the fried debla to a paper towel–lined colander and let it drain. Repeat with the remaining dough.

3   Place the remaining ingredients and 1½ cups water in a saucepan, cover the pan, and simmer the mixture over low heat until it is a thick syrup, about 45 minutes. Stir the syrup and remove the pan from heat.

4   Dip the debla into the warm syrup, soaking them well. Place them in a colander and let them drain.

5   When the syrup has cooled and hardened, arrange the debla on a serving platter and enjoy.

YIELD: **8 SERVINGS**

ACTIVE TIME: **30 MINUTES**

TOTAL TIME: **1 HOUR AND 30 MINUTES**

Cardamom Biscotti

INGREDIENTS

1½ cups all-purpose flour

¾ teaspoon baking powder

Pinch of fine sea salt

¼ cup sugar

⅓ cup light brown sugar

¾ teaspoon cardamom

½ teaspoon cinnamon

¼ teaspoon ground ginger

⅛ teaspoon ground cloves

⅛ teaspoon freshly grated nutmeg

Zest of 1 orange

2 eggs

¼ cup extra-virgin olive oil

1 teaspoon pure vanilla extract

DIRECTIONS

1   Preheat the oven to 350°F. Line a baking sheet with parchment paper. Place all of the ingredients, except for the orange zest, eggs, olive oil, and vanilla, in a mixing bowl and whisk until combined.

2   Add the remaining ingredients and work the mixture by hand until it comes together as a smooth dough. Roll the dough into a log that is about 6 inches long and about 2 inches wide. Place the log on the baking sheet, place it in the oven, and bake until golden brown, about 20 minutes.

3   Remove the biscotti from the oven and let it cool.

4   Cut the biscotti into the desired shape and size. Place the biscotti back in the oven and bake until crispy, about 20 minutes.

5   Remove the biscotti from the oven, transfer to a wire rack, and let them cool completely before enjoying.

Pignoli

INGREDIENTS

1¾ cups unsweetened almond paste, plus 1 teaspoon

1½ cups confectioners' sugar

2 tablespoons honey

Pinch of cinnamon

Pinch of fine sea salt

2 large egg whites, at room temperature

Zest of 1 lemon

¾ cup pine nuts

DIRECTIONS

1 Preheat the oven to 350°F and line two baking sheets with parchment paper. In the work bowl of a stand mixer fitted with the paddle attachment, beat the almond paste until it is thoroughly broken up. Add the confectioners' sugar and beat the mixture on low until combined.

2 Add the honey, cinnamon, salt, egg whites, and lemon zest, raise the speed to medium, and beat until the mixture is very thick, about 5 minutes.

3 Drop tablespoons of dough onto the prepared baking sheets and gently pat pine nuts into each of the cookies. Place the cookies in the oven and bake until golden brown, 12 to 14 minutes. Remove from the oven and let the cookies cool on the baking sheets.

METRIC CONVERSIONS

U.S. Measurement	Approximate Metric Liquid Measurement	Approximate Metric Dry Measurement
1 teaspoon	5 ml	5 g
1 tablespoon or ½ ounce	15 ml	14 g
1 ounce or ⅛ cup	30 ml	29 g
¼ cup or 2 ounces	60 ml	57 g
⅓ cup	80 ml	76 g
½ cup or 4 ounces	120 ml	113 g
⅔ cup	160 ml	151 g
¾ cup or 6 ounces	180 ml	170 g
1 cup or 8 ounces or ½ pint	240 ml	227 g
1½ cups or 12 ounces	350 ml	340 g
2 cups or 1 pint or 16 ounces	475 ml	454 g
3 cups or 1½ pints	700 ml	680 g
4 cups or 2 pints or 1 quart	950 ml	908 g

INDEX

ABOUT CIDER MILL PRESS BOOK PUBLISHERS

Good ideas ripen with time. From seed to harvest, Cider Mill Press brings fine reading, information, and entertainment together between the covers of its creatively crafted books. Our Cider Mill bears fruit twice a year, publishing a new crop of titles each spring and fall.

"Where Good Books Are Ready for Press"

Visit us online at
cidermillpress.com

or write to us at
PO Box 454
12 Spring St.
Kennebunkport, Maine 04046